D0352581

50 WALKS IN

Oxfordshire

50 WALKS OF 2–10 MILES

9000001000 4 971

First published 2003
Researched and written by Nick Channer and Ann F Stonehouse
Field checked and updated 2008 by David Hancock and Nick Reynolds
Series Management: Bookwork Creative Associates
Series Editors: Sandy Draper and Marilynne Lanng
Series design concept: Elizabeth Baldin and Andrew Milne
Designer: Elizabeth Baldin
Picture Research: Liz Stacey
Proofreader: Pamela Stagg
Cartography provided by the Mapping Services Department of AA Publishing

Produced by AA Publishing
© Automobile Association Developments Limited 2009

Published by AA Publishing (a trading name of Automobile Association Developments Limited,
whose registered office is Fanum House, Basing View, Basingstoke, Hampshire RG21 4EA;
registered number 1878835)

  This product includes mapping data licensed from the Ordnance
Survey® with the permission of the Controller of Her Majesty's
Stationery Office. © Crown Copyright 2009. All rights reserved. Licence number 100021153.

A03627

ISBN: 978-0-7495-6057-7

A CIP catalogue record for this book is available from the British Library.

The contents of this book are believed correct at the time of printing. Nevertheless, the
publishers cannot be held responsible for any errors or omissions or for changes in the
details given in this book or for the consequences of any reliance on the information it
provides. This does not affect your statutory rights. We have tried to ensure accuracy in this
book, but things do change and we would be grateful if readers would advise us of any
inaccuracies they may encounter.

We have taken all reasonable steps to ensure that these walks are safe and achievable by
walkers with a realistic level of fitness. However, all outdoor activities involve a degree of risk
and the publishers accept no responsibility for any injuries caused to readers whilst following
these walks. For more advice on walking safely see page 144. The mileage range shown on the
front cover is for guidance only – some walks may be less than or exceed these distances.

Visit AA Publishing at www.aatravelshop.com

Colour reproduction by Keenes Group, Andover
Printed by Printer Trento Srl, Italy

Acknowledgements
The Automobile Association would like to thank the following photographers, companies and
picture libraries for their assistance in the preparation of this book.

Abbreviations for the picture credits are as follows: (t) top; (b) bottom; (l) left; (r) right; (AA)
AA World Travel Library.

3 © Barry Hitchcox/Alamy; 9 AA/D Hall; 12/3 AA/V Greaves; 32/3 AA/C Jones; 48/9 © Phil
Ball/Rex Features; 64/5 AA/H Palmer; 84/5 AA/S Day; 104/5 AA/M Short; 121 AA/D Hall;
122 AA/D Hall.

Every effort has been made to trace the copyright holders, and we apologise in advance for
any accidental errors. We would be happy to apply the corrections in the following edition of
this publication.

Right: A field of wild poppies at Faringdon (Walk 18)

50 WALKS IN

Oxfordshire

50 WALKS OF 2–10 MILES

Contents

Contents

Rating

Each walk is rated for its relative difficulty compared to the other walks in this book. Walks marked +++ are likely to be shorter and easier with little total ascent. The hardest walks are marked +++

Walking in Safety

For advice and safety tips see page 144.

Locator Map

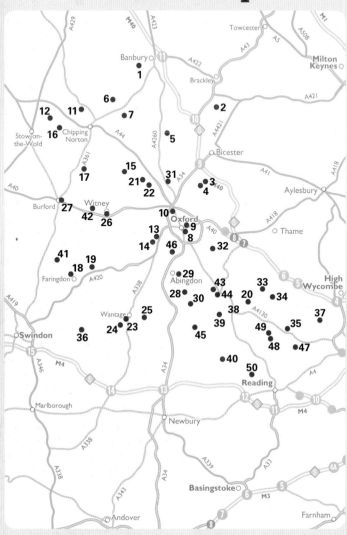

Legend

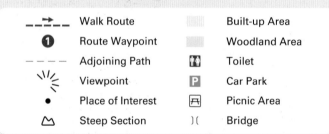

⇢ Walk Route		▨ Built-up Area	
❶ Route Waypoint		▨ Woodland Area	
– – – Adjoining Path		👫 Toilet	
☀ Viewpoint		🅿 Car Park	
• Place of Interest		⊟ Picnic Area	
⌂ Steep Section		)(Bridge	

6

Introducing Oxfordshire

Located at the heart of England, Oxfordshire enjoys a rich heritage and surprisingly varied scenery. Its landscape encompasses open chalk downland and glorious beechwoods, picturesque rivers and attractive villages set in peaceful farmland. In the south-west the county meets Berkshire high on the downs, and here there are far-reaching vistas and fascinating links with the ancient past. To the south-east lie the Chilterns, their steep scarps and tree-clad hills providing a superb natural playground in this densely populated area. The countryside in the north-west of Oxfordshire seems isolated by comparison, more redolent of the north of England, with its broad views, undulating landscape and dry-stone walls.

Shaping Oxfordshire

The county demonstrates how the strong influence of humans has shaped this part of England over the centuries. The Romans built villas in the pretty river valleys that thread their way through Oxfordshire, the Saxons constructed royal palaces here, and the Normans left an impressive legacy of castles and churches. The philanthropic wool merchants made their mark too, and many of their fine buildings serve as a long-lasting testimony to what they did for the good of the local community.

Like many of the English counties, Oxfordshire has witnessed its battles over the years – it was stained by the blood of the Danes in the 9th century AD and ravaged by the armies of the English Civil War. The struggle for power and political supremacy has produced some of history's most prominent figures. One of Oxfordshire's boldest sons, Alfred the Great, was born at Wantage, while Winston Churchill, the man who symbolised Britain's fighting spirit during the Second World War, will always be associated with Blenheim Palace, his family home and now one of Britain's greatest visitor attractions.

River Thames

The majestic Thames has been described as liquid history. Rising in a Gloucestershire meadow, the fledgling river drifts towards Oxford, then heads south through Abingdon, Wallingford and Goring. In its own way Britain's most famous river has helped mould the county's distinctive character through the centuries.

PUBLIC TRANSPORT

Oxfordshire is well served by public transport, making many of the walks in this guide easily accessible. For information about bus services contact Traveline on 0870 608 2 608. Walks 5, 8, 9, 10, 17, 30, 39 and 40 start at or near a railway station. For times of trains throughout the country, call the 24-hour national train enquiry line on 08457 48 49 50. For countrywide public transport information look at the internet site www.pti.org.uk.

Oxfordshire has two national trails – the gentle Thames Path and the timeless Ridgeway. Both routes, parts of which appear in this guide, explore the rural heart of the county, giving a unique insight into the changing face of the countryside. Elsewhere Oxfordshire is criss-crossed by a network of ancient paths and tracks. Different generations followed these routes to work in fields and factories, or to go to school, market and church.

Towns and Cities

Towns and cities are a feature of this book, too. The sleepy backwaters of Abingdon, Wallingford, Wantage, Watlington and Witney reveal how these old towns evolved over the centuries, while Oxford's imposing streets reflect the beauty and elegance of 'that sweet city with her dreaming spires.' Fans of the fictional sleuth Inspector Morse will recognise many Oxford landmarks described in the books and used in the television series.

Each route offers a specific theme to enhance the walk, as well as snippets of useful information on what to look for and what to do while you're there. Visitor attractions crop up on many routes; to avoid disappointment, find out opening times and if dogs are welcome before setting out. Apart from two walks, which require a train to return to the start, all are circular.

Using this book

INFORMATION PANELS

An information panel for each walk shows its relative difficulty (see Page 5), the distance and total amount of ascent. An indication of the gradients you will encounter is shown by the rating ▲ ▲ ▲ (no steep slopes) to ▲ ▲ ▲ (several very steep slopes).

MAPS

There are 30 maps, covering 40 of the walks. Some walks have a suggested option in the same area. The information panel for these walks will tell you how much extra walking is involved. On short-cut suggestions the panel will tell you the total distance if you set out from the start of the main walk. Where an option returns to the same point on the main walk, just the distance of the loop is given. Where an option leaves the main walk at one point and returns to it at another, then the distance shown is for the whole walk. The minimum time suggested is for reasonably fit walkers and doesn't allow for stops. Each walk has a suggested map.

START POINTS

The start of each walk is given as a six-figure grid reference prefixed by two letters indicating which 100km square of the National Grid it refers to. You'll find more information on grid references on most Ordnance Survey maps.

DOGS

We have tried to give dog owners useful advice about how dog friendly each walk is. Please respect other countryside users. Keep your dog under control, especially around livestock, and obey local bylaws and other dog control notices.

CAR PARKING

Many of the car parks suggested are public, but occasionally you may find you have to park on the roadside or in a lay-by. Please be considerate when you leave your car, ensuring that access roads or gates are not blocked and that other vehicles can pass safely.

Right: Kelmscott Manor (Walk 41)

Broughton's Magnificent Moated Castle

Take a delightful walk across open country and through fine parkland to a splendid Tudor pile.

DISTANCE 2.75 miles (4.4km)   **MINIMUM TIME** 1hr 30min

ASCENT/GRADIENT 82ft (25m) ▲▲▲   **LEVEL OF DIFFICULTY** ✦✦✦

PATHS Field and parkland paths and tracks, some roads, 5 stiles

LANDSCAPE Rolling farmland and parkland to south-west of Banbury

SUGGESTED MAP OS Explorer 191 Banbury, Bicester & Chipping Norton

START/FINISH Grid reference: SP 421384

DOG FRIENDLINESS Under control across farmland and by Broughton Castle

PARKING Limited spaces in Broughton village

PUBLIC TOILETS Broughton Castle, for visitors; otherwise none en route

---

One of the pleasures of walking in the countryside is that initial glimpse of a ruined church, a wonderfully eccentric folly or a distant baronial hall. The first sighting of Broughton Castle usually provokes a gasp of surprise, too, as it edges teasingly into view across an extensive swathe of green lawns and classic English parkland.

The castle was originally built as a fortified manor house by Sir John de Broughton early in the 14th century. Later it passed to William de Wykeham, the famous founding father of Winchester College and New College, Oxford, who set about converting the manor house into a castle, designing battlements and a gatehouse among other additions. One of Broughton's greatest attributes is its 14th-century private chapel, approached by a stone staircase from the groined passage.

In the 15th century, Broughton passed by marriage to the Fiennes family when the granddaughter of Sir Thomas Wykeham, great-nephew and heir of William, married William Fiennes, 2nd Lord Saye and Sele. During the Elizabethan era the house was transformed virtually beyond recognition into the Tudor building you see today.

Subtle Support

During the Civil War, the Fiennes family were staunch supporters of the Parliamentarians and did much to defend this corner of Oxfordshire. The 1st Viscount Saye and Sele, demonstrating caution and common sense, was dubbed 'Old Subtlety', and it was within the walls of the castle, in the Council Chamber, that Puritan leaders such as Pym, Hampden, Vane and Essex met to plot the Great Rebellion and thwart Charles I. Saye and Sele raised his own regiment of dragoons, known as Lord Saye's Bluecoats after the colour of their uniform, from among his tenantry. Together with his four sons, he fought at the Battle of Edgehill in 1642, but soon afterwards the castle was besieged and captured. The distinctive compound title of Saye and Sele dates from the original creation of the barony in 1447.

Members of the Fiennes dynasty still live at Broughton Castle, which is open to the public (not daily – check for opening times), and today the name takes on even greater significance. Ralph and Joseph, both well-known and well-respected film and stage actors, are members of the family.

Not surprisingly, the castle often crops up as an imposing backdrop in film and television productions. Perhaps most notable on the list of credits is the 1998 film *Shakespeare in Love* (with Joseph Fiennes as William Shakespeare) in which Broughton Castle appears as Viola's stately home. The dance, where Will first meets her, was filmed in the Great Hall, with its beautiful plaster ceiling and hanging bosses, while it is in the Oak Room that Wessex tells Viola that she is to be married. For outdoor scenes, an artificial balcony, overlooking formal gardens, was constructed, representing part of Viola's bedroom.

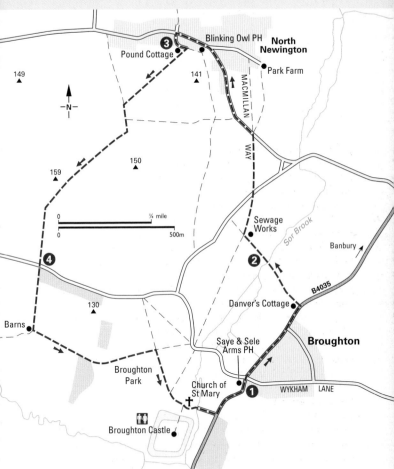

WALK 1 DIRECTIONS

1 Keep Wykham Lane on your right and parkland on the left and walk through the village of Broughton. Pass Danvers Road on the right-hand side, followed by Danvers Cottage on the left and, when the road curves right just beyond the cottage, swing left over a stile, signposted 'North Newington'. Keep ahead across the field to reach a stile in the next boundary, then keep left

Overleaf: Broughton Castle reflected in its moat, Banbury

around the field-edge to cross a footbridge in the trees. This is sometimes obscured by foliage during the summer months. Continue ahead, keeping a line of trees on your right-hand side and, three-quarters of the way along the field boundary, look for a footbridge on the right.

WHERE TO EAT AND DRINK

The Saye and Sele Arms in Broughton is a popular, characterful pub offering everything from sandwiches to steaks. As well as the dining area, there is a garden where you can relax over a drink after the walk. The pub is closed on Sunday evenings. The Blinking Owl at North Newington is cosy on a cold winter's day, and has traditional ales and a good menu. There is a tea room at Broughton Castle.

2 Cross the footbridge, followed by a concrete track, to reach another stile, and head diagonally left across the field to a minor road. Take the right of way on the opposite side and follow a stretch of the Macmillan Way across a field to reach a stile. Cross the stile to the lane and turn left. Walk towards the village of North Newington, passing the entrance to Park Farm on your right-hand side. Pass the Blinking Owl pub and Wheelwright Cottage and then turn left into The Pound, opposite the old village pump.

3 Walk past Pound Cottage and look for a footpath which starts about 30yds (27m) beyond it on the right-hand side. Follow the footpath diagonally right across the field to reach a wide, obvious gap in the hedgerow on the far side. Turn left to reach another gap in the hedge, then head obliquely right in the field,

WHILE YOU'RE THERE

Visit Banbury, the second largest town in Oxfordshire, renowned for its historic buildings and different architectural styles. Banbury's museum occupies an attractive canalside setting and its modern displays illustrate the town's origins and colourful past.

making for the top corner, which is defined by trees and hedgerow. Pass through the gate and keep ahead, with the field boundary on your immediate left. Walk along to the next gate and then down the field to the road.

4 Cross the road to a galvanised gate and follow the track towards some barns. Keep to the left of these buildings and look for a stile and footpath branching off to the left, passing beside two sheds on your left. Follow the path to reach a stile in the far boundary and cross over into the parkland of Broughton Castle. Soon the spire of Broughton church and the outline of the castle and its moat come into sight ahead of you. Continue ahead across the parkland and down to meet the castle drive. Head for a gate into the churchyard and then follow a path to reach the B4035 on the outskirts of Broughton. Turn left along the road and return to the start of the walk in the village centre.

WHAT TO LOOK OUT FOR

As you cross the parkland towards Broughton Castle, look for the spire of Broughton's Church of St Mary, its imposing tower crowned by a fine spire. The church dates mainly from the 14th century and includes an elaborate painted tomb of Sir John de Broughton.

From Cottisford to Juniper Hill

Visit two villages vividly brought to life through the books of the remarkable local writer, Flora Thompson.

DISTANCE 3.75 miles (6km))   **MINIMUM TIME** 1hr 45min

ASCENT/GRADIENT 90ft (27m) ▲▲▲   **LEVEL OF DIFFICULTY** ✦✦✦

PATHS Tracks, field paths, stretches of quiet country roads, 2 stiles

LANDSCAPE Quiet farmland to south of Brackley

SUGGESTED MAP OS Explorer 191 Banbury, Bicester & Chipping Norton

START/FINISH Grid reference: SP 591312

DOG FRIENDLINESS On lead in Cottisford and Juniper Hill and near pheasants

PARKING Restricted parking in Cottisford

PUBLIC TOILETS None en route

Flora June Timms was one of thousands of children growing up in rural north-east Oxfordshire in the latter part of the 19th century. But Flora was blessed with a rare gift. She had an observant eye and a sharp awareness of her surroundings. As a girl, she studied the daily routine closely – the minutiae of everyday life in a traditional English village.

Magical Memories

Years later, as Flora Thompson, a married woman in her sixties, she began writing sketches of her precious childhood which later became the basis for three famous books – *Lark Rise* (Juniper Hill), *Over to Candleford* (an amalgam of nearby Banbury, Bicester and Buckingham) and *Candleford Green*. The stories were published during the Second World War and then in 1945 as a trilogy – *Lark Rise to Candleford*. Even today her work is seen as a brilliantly crafted social record of the times, expertly capturing the spirit and essence of rural life during the closing stages of the Victorian era.

A Country Childhood

Flora was born at Juniper Hill in 1876, the eldest of ten children. Her father was a stonemason who worked in Brackley and her mother had been employed locally as a nursemaid. From the age of seven, Flora attended the local school at neighbouring Cottisford. She walked there and back from Juniper Hill with other children from the village. 'Up the long, straight road they straggled, in twos and threes and in gangs, their flat, rush dinner-baskets over their shoulders and their shabby coats on their arms against the rain.' Every Sunday Flora attended church at Cottisford with her brother Edwin, sitting in their grandfather's pew opposite the door. At the age of 14, she left school and went to work as a post office assistant at nearby Fringford. It proved to be a good move for young Flora. She made use of her employer's library, developing and expanding her knowledge and understanding of literature. Mrs Whitton 'had more influence than anyone in shaping the outward course of my life', she wrote.

COTTISFORD

Flora's Rise to Fame

At the age of 20, Flora left Juniper Hill to work at a post office in Surrey. She later moved to Essex and then to Hampshire, where she met and married John Thompson, a junior post office clerk. They had three children, Winifred, Basil and Peter. In 1928 John became postmaster in Dartmouth. Now firmly established in the West Country, Flora began writing, recalling the days of her childhood in Juniper Hill. But tragedy was to overwhelm Flora. During the Second World War, her younger son, Peter, joined the Merchant Navy and was killed when his ship was torpedoed. Flora never fully recovered from the shock.

A Fitting Tribute

After the war, having written *Still Glides the Stream* – her final work – Flora developed pneumonia, which left her with a weak heart. She died in 1947, aged 70. A festival was held at Cottisford in 1976 to mark her centenary and two years later a stage version of *Lark Rise* was performed by the National Theatre. In 2007 the BBC showed a serialised version of *Lark Rise to Candleford*.

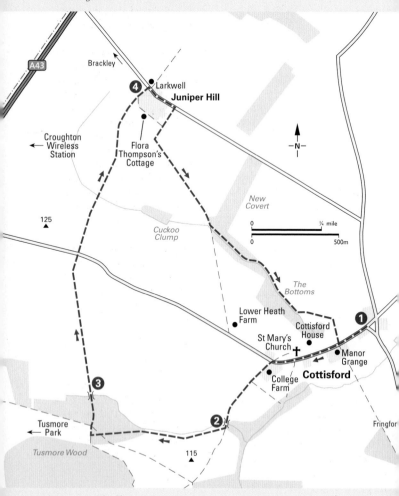

COTTISFORD

WALK 2 DIRECTIONS

1 Keep the postbox and telephone box on the right and follow the road through Cottisford. Pass the church on your right and, when the road swings round to the right, branch left at the entrance to College Farm. Keep the farm outbuildings on your left and follow the track, which runs between tall hedges. Continue to a gap in the hedgerow on the right and turn right to join a bridleway.

2 Keep trees, a ditch and a hedgerow on your right-hand side and, further on, the bridleway cuts between margins of bracken. Pass alongside a plantation to reach a junction with a track. Turn right and walk along to a left bend, with the buildings of Tusmore Park visible to your left. Swing right here to join a waymarked footpath, then bear left almost immediately. Keep alongside a wire fence and, on reaching the corner, go straight ahead over a footbridge.

3 Head north, keeping trees and hedgerow on the right, and eventually you come to a track. Go straight on to reach some double wooden gates and a stile. Cross the road beyond and take the path on the opposite side signposted to Juniper. Follow

the right of way leading across the fields. Over to the left, in the distance, are the dishes of Croughton Wireless Station. Approaching Juniper Hill, join a drive serving bungalows. Keep ahead to the road and turn right opposite a cottage called Larkwell.

4 Pass the former village inn, the Fox, and continue along the road as far as the village sign for Juniper Hill. Turn right just beyond it at the sign for Cottisford. Follow the path which runs between allotments, then cross a stile and head diagonally left across a large field, making for a curtain of woodland in the distance. Look for a track in the corner and cut between trees to the next field. Keep right, alongside the edge of the woodland, with a ditch just beside you. Cross into the next field and continue all the way to meet the road. Turn left opposite Manor Grange and return to the centre of Cottisford and the start of the walk.

Bewitched Otmoor – the Forgotten Land

Explore a desolate landscape, perhaps more reminiscent of the East Anglian fens than Oxfordshire.

DISTANCE 3.5 miles (5.6km) **MINIMUM TIME** 1hr 30min

ASCENT/GRADIENT Negligible ▲▲▲ **LEVEL OF DIFFICULTY** ✦✦✦

PATHS Country road, tracks and paths

LANDSCAPE Remote wetland and farmland

SUGGESTED MAP OS Explorer 180 Oxford

START/FINISH Grid reference: SP 563157

DOG FRIENDLINESS Under control in vicinity of firing range. On lead on alternative linking paths across Otmoor

PARKING Spaces near church at Charlton-on-Otmoor

PUBLIC TOILETS None en route

A stone's throw to the north of Oxford lies Otmoor, a canvas of fields and hedgerows that seems to have been bypassed by the rest of the county. A curious ghostly stillness pervades this wilderness, inspiring various writers over the years to describe it romantically as 'the forgotten land', 'bewitched Otmoor' and 'sleeping Otmoor cast under a spell of ancient magic.'

An Abandoned Landscape

Some of it is sheltered and here you can savour the rural charm of green lanes and quiet woodland. Now and again there are signs of life too – the rifle range and the seven villages scattered on various elevations overlooking the perimeter of the moor. The residents once used Otmoor's unpromising terrain for grazing cattle and for wildfowling, fishing and collecting fuel. But mostly it is an austere, abandoned landscape over which the passage of time has had little influence.

With its flat fields, ditches and dykes, it is, in places, reminiscent of East Anglia. On a cold winter's day, and even occasionally in high summer, you can sense Otmoor's sinister, sometimes unsettling, atmosphere. At times it is dark and mysterious, at times it exudes an air of calm and tranquillity. Cross Otmoor as a light mist drifts over the meadows and you'll find the image will linger long in the memory.

Alice's Giant Chessboard

If time allows, journey to the village of Beckley, perched 400ft (122m) over the southern edge of Otmoor, and you'll see why Lewis Carroll was supposedly inspired by the view of this primitive 4,000-acre (1,620ha) landscape to write about the giant chessboard in *Alice Through the Looking Glass*. John Buchan, who lived at nearby Elsfield, described Otmoor in great detail in his novel *The Blanket of the Dark*.

Centuries ago, Otmoor was waterlogged during much of the year. However, by the late 1820s the moor had been drained and enclosed for agricultural use, as a result of the efforts of landowners. But this was met with fierce opposition from the local commoners, leading to serious rioting in the area. The rioters, who for so long had been allowed to graze livestock on the common land of Otmoor, moved in and destroyed new fences, hedges, gates and bridges. But it was a pointless exercise.

Police and troops were drafted in to help tackle the problem and eventually the rioters acknowledged defeat and withdrew. Nearly 50 local villagers were arrested and taken to Oxford, which happened to be staging its annual St Giles' Fair. The crowds sided with the rioters, shouting 'Otmoor for ever'.

Paradise Reprieved

In the 1980s the moor was at the centre of a bitter row once again, when it was under threat from a proposal to build a new motorway extension. After much opposition, the threat was lifted in order to accommodate a rare butterfly whose breeding ground is Otmoor. In fact the whole area is a paradise for birders and botanists, and there are many species of birds and plants to be found in the RSPB reserve in the heart of Otmoor. Besides the various resident bird species, many more pass through on a fly-line from the Severn to the Wash.

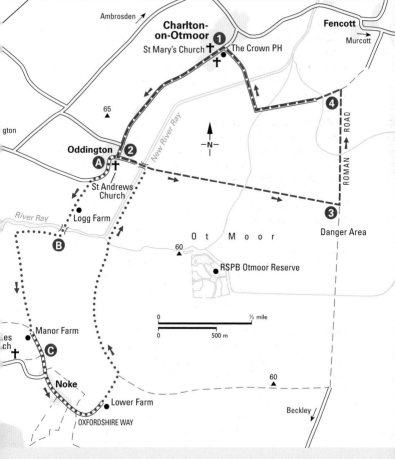

WALK 3

WALK 3 DIRECTIONS

1 Keep the church on the right and walk through the village of Charlton-on-Otmoor. Pass Blacksmiths Lane and continue on the road out of the village. Follow the lane between hedgerows and fields. Soon you reach the sign for Oddington. When the road bends right, branch off to the left by the bus shelter and turn left just past the telephone box on to a track.

WHAT TO LOOK OUT FOR

There is a military firing range on Otmoor. Look for written information about the range at the side of the path and follow the advice carefully. The Emperor moth, marsh fritillary butterflies and Black Hairstreak are among a number of rare insects found on Otmoor. Take a walk across the moor and you may find the landscape partially puckered with holes from the Second World War bombing practice.

2 Take the track out of the village, crossing a concrete bridge after a short walk. At the next junction, just beyond it, avoid the galvanised gates on the right, and follow the parallel bridleway, cutting between ditches and hedges. (It can be very wet during the winter months so it may be best to take the parallel bridleway through the gates and later join the bridleway when you reach Otmoor RSPB Reserve.) Eventually, pass a stile on the left, leading to a linking path which provides an alternative route to the wetlands of Otmoor. The tower of Charlton-on-Otmoor church can be seen at intervals along the track. Continue to the signs for Otmoor's military firing range. Keep ahead until you reach a gate on the left and several gates on the right.

3 Turn left at this point and follow the old Roman road north. The track is broad and can be wet in winter. When it curves right, branch off to the left and begin the last leg of the walk.

WHILE YOU'RE THERE

St Mary's Church at Charlton-on-Otmoor is a fine medieval building with a tall tower which is a useful landmark when walking on Otmoor. The building is Grade I listed and mentioned in the book *England's 1000 Best Churches* by Simon Jenkins.

4 Follow the path through the trees and soon it broadens to a track cutting between fields and hedgerows. There are good views across a broad expanse of Otmoor to the south. Cross a wooden footbridge and continue on the track. Turn right by some corrugated barns and make for Charlton-on-Otmoor. The church tower is clearly visible now. Cross the New River Ray and climb the slope to the junction. Turn left by the Crown and return to the church in the centre of the village.

WHERE TO EAT AND DRINK

The Crown in Charlton-on-Otmoor serves meals and traditional bar food. The only pub on the walk, The Crown benefits from a popular beer garden. Many of the pubs in the nearby villages serve food, including the Nut Tree Inn at Murcott, the Abingdon Arms at Beckley and the Red Lion at Islip.

Noke – at the Oak Trees

Make for a sleepy village hidden along the edge of Otmoor.

See map and information panel for Walk 3

DISTANCE 7 miles (11.3km)	MINIMUM TIME 3hrs
ASCENT/GRADIENT Negligible ▲▲▲	LEVEL OF DIFFICULTY +++

WALK 4 DIRECTIONS
(Walk 3 option)

Keep to the road following it right, then left through the village, Point **Ⓐ**. On the left is Oddington church, whose past rectors include Gilbert Sheldon (1598–1677). Sheldon was appointed Bishop of London in 1660 and Archbishop of Canterbury three years later. He became Chancellor at Oxford and also donated £12,200 to build the city's Sheldonian Theatre.

Pass the church and continue along the lane. Look for a path, hidden by foliage in summer, beyond the next bend in the road, and go through a dilapidated kissing gate. After several paces, the path reaches the corner of a field. Cut diagonally right across it towards the far corner, making for the end of a line of trees. Keep to the right of Logg Farm, join a drive for a few paces, then swing right at the waymark, following a track. As it curves left towards a detached house, go straight on along a fenced grassy track, passing under power lines. Cross a track to a stile and keep to the left field boundary, looking for a footbridge in the corner.

Cross the River Ray, Point **Ⓑ**, to a second footbridge and turn right to skirt the field-edge. Keep the water on your right and approach a gap in the field boundary. Keep this side of it, turn left and head south, keeping the hedge on your immediate right. Join a track by a circular tank and keep ahead. Follow the right of way between hedgerows, and veer left at a fork. Where the track curves right towards Manor Farm, go straight on along a grassy path left of the outbuildings. Head for a junction of paths and go straight on to the road, Point **Ⓒ**.

Keep left, pass Rectory Cottage and walk through Noke (meaning 'at the oak trees'), avoiding a path to Woodeaton. The font at St Giles Church was given by the lady of the manor, Gundreda, a daughter of William the Conqueror.

Continue on the lane, passing a sign for Lower Farm. Follow the drive towards the farm buildings, branching left before them at the fork. Follow the track to a bridge and junction opposite double gates, turn left and follow the grassy track. Cross a sluice gate, then follow the clear track to the next junction by a bridge and galvanised gates. Turn right and rejoin Walk 3 just after Point **❷**.

Rousham's Classic Garden

A walk that includes a delightful garden and a stretch of inland waterway.

DISTANCE 5 miles (8km)   **MINIMUM TIME** 2hrs

ASCENT/GRADIENT 150ft (46m) ▲▲▲   **LEVEL OF DIFFICULTY** ✦✦✦

PATHS Field paths, tow path and road (can be busy), 4 stiles

LANDSCAPE Pretty countryside with Oxford Canal and River Cherwell

SUGGESTED MAP OS Explorer 191 Banbury, Bicester & Chipping Norton

START/FINISH Grid reference: SP 476262

DOG FRIENDLINESS Under control on tow path

PARKING Recreation ground car park at Steeple Aston

PUBLIC TOILETS Rousham House, for visitors; otherwise none en route

WALK 5 DIRECTIONS

From the car park, turn left and walk down the street (Paines Hill) through the village of Steeple Aston to the T-junction. The post office and shop are on the corner and across the way is the White Lion pub. Turn right into South Side and pass Jubilee Close. Carry on ahead until you see a tarmac drive on the left, opposite Radley Cottage. Follow it as it dwindles to a track that heads south. When it runs into a field, continue ahead on a waymarked path cutting across fields. Make for a gap in the hedgerow and follow the path through the undergrowth, across a stile and down into the next field.

Keep woodland over to the left and aim for the far left corner of the field and a stile leading out to the road. Cross over and go up the bank, turning left at the top. Follow the path through the trees to a stile leading into a large field. Cross it diagonally, making for a gate by farm buildings. Exit to the road and turn right to visit Rousham House or left to continue the walk.

The lovely Cherwell Valley is the perfect setting for this splendid mansion. Built by Sir Robert Dormer in 1635, on an H-plan, the house was remodelled by William Kent just over 100 years later with an air of free Gothic style about it. Kent was a coach-painter's apprentice who became an architect and landscape gardener. He designed Horse Guards, the famous London landmark, in 1745.

The garden at Rousham is a lasting monument to the work of Kent and a fine example of English landscape design. Here,

WHERE TO EAT AND DRINK

Picnicking is permitted within the gardens of Rousham House. If you prefer pubs, try the White Lion at Steeple Aston, or the Bell at Lower Heyford, which dates back to 1602. There is also Kizzies, a waterside café/bistro by the canal at Heyford Wharf.

the River Cherwell flows through 30 acres (12ha) of garden, which has more than a hint of the Italianate. Among the many features are cascades and ponds, groves, the Temple of Echo and the seven-arched portico known as Praeneste. No wonder Horace Walpole called it 'Kentissimo'.

A peaceful stroll along Long Walk is one of Rousham's most popular attractions, and inside the house there are many treasures too, including a panelled oak chamber and a painted parlour, originally a small 17th-century kitchen.

As you leave Rousham, walk along to the church located in a peaceful setting a short distance from the main house. Enter the churchyard and at once there is a poignant reminder of the sheer futility of the First World War. On the right are the graves of two young men killed in battle, members of the Cottrell-Dormer family of Rousham House.

Follow the road down to the traffic-lights and turn right just beyond them. Cross the River Cherwell and look to your right for a splendid view of Rousham House framed by trees. Pass the entrance to Heyford railway station and follow the road over the railway and the parallel Oxford Canal. Turn left immediately beyond it, by Canal Cottage, and follow the path back over the canal to join the tow path. Look for the tower of Lower Heyford church and keep ahead to a swing bridge, which allows access to the village.

Continue on the tow path for a mile (1.6km), pass Allen's Lock and make for bridge No 203. Turn left up the bank and turn left across the river bridge, then veer right in the field to a bridge over the river. Keep the water on your right and look for a railway embankment ahead. Pass under the railway bridge and cross the field to a footbridge and stile set against a curtain of trees.

Go up the bank and the field slope towards trees in the top boundary. Cut through them into the next field, keeping right here. The Rousham Eyecatcher is a useful directional landmark at this point. Alone and forgotten in the middle of a field, again the work of William Kent, its sudden appearance on the brow of the hill catches you by surprise. The Eyecatcher is a buttressed three-arched ruin or sham, instantly reminiscent of a castle gateway and visible on the skyline – hence the name. Like follies, they were once fashionable with whimsical landowners and colourful eccentrics. The Rousham Eyecatcher's solitary position makes it hard to find for anyone other than those passing this way on foot. Nevertheless, it consolidates Kent's undisputed creative genius.

Follow the boundary down and round to a gate. Join a track and turn right. Head up to the edge of Steeple Aston, go right at the junction and return to the car park at the start.

WHILE YOU'RE THERE

Make a detour to Lower Heyford, formerly Heyford Purcell, after the Purcell family who moved here from nearby Newton Purcell. The village was once an important river crossing on the Cherwell, especially at hay harvest time – the name is probably derived from 'hay ford'. The stone bridge replaced the ford and was constructed during the 13th century.

Hook Norton's Towering Success

Explore delightful ironstone country before visiting one of Oxfordshire's more unusual buildings.

WALK 6

DISTANCE 4.5 miles (7.2km)	**MINIMUM TIME** 2hrs

ASCENT/GRADIENT 164ft (50m) ▲▲▲　**LEVEL OF DIFFICULTY** ✦✦✦

PATHS Field paths, tracks and bridleways, quiet roads

LANDSCAPE Undulating countryside close to Warwickshire border

SUGGESTED MAP OS Explorer 191 Banbury, Bicester & Chipping Norton

START/FINISH Grid reference: SP 355331

DOG FRIENDLINESS Under control on farmland and on lead where requested

PARKING Spaces in Hook Norton village centre

PUBLIC TOILETS Hook Norton Brewery Visitor Centre

Hook Norton is one of those places that you are most likely to stumble upon by accident. Hidden away down winding lanes a few miles from the Cotswold town of Chipping Norton, this sizeable village, one of the largest parishes in Oxfordshire, is typical of many other settlements in the county – with one possible exception.

Tucked away in Brewery Lane, on the edge of the village, is the Hook Norton Brewery, displaying one of the most distinctive and unusual Victorian façades in the country. The tower brewing building, erected at the turn of the last century, has been described as 'an essay in brick, ironstone, slate, weather-boarding, half timber and cast iron.'

Following Tradition

During the 19th century it was traditional for most towns, cities and even large villages to have their own brewery. During the 1880s Oxfordshire alone had almost 50. Today, the scarcity of independent breweries reflects the changing fortunes of the licensed trade. However, the Hook Norton Brewery has managed to fight off the big corporate companies and it remains successful.

It was during the Victorian era, in 1849, that John Harris set up in business as a maltster by brewing beer in a nearby farmhouse. A year later, Harris built his own brewhouse, where he used pure Cotswold spring water. He soon found there was a great demand for his beer and so he established a small brewery with its own maltings.

Growing the Business

When Harris died, his son and nephew assumed responsibility for the running of the business and by 1899 work on the present tower brewery was complete. The new building, comprising six floors, housed the latest brewing equipment and allowed the entire brewing sequence to be undertaken as a continuous process. It was at this time that John Harris and Company became the Hook Norton Brewery Company Limited. Following the death of John Harris, the task of running the brewery fell to his son-in-

HOOK NORTON

law Alban Clarke, who was killed in a motorcycle accident in 1917. Hook Norton remains a family business in the 21st century. The brewery is now run by James Clarke, Alban Clarke's great, great grandson.

There is nothing brash or hi-tech about Hook Norton. Much of the brewery's intricate machinery is original – the process of brewing has been the same for over 100 years and apart from a new laboratory, stainless-steel copper and cooling system, little has changed. One of the brewery's greatest assets is the mighty steam-driven, 25-horse-power piston engine, dating back to 1899. Today the Hook Norton Brewery has 47 tied houses and its beers supply around 300 free trade pubs. In September 1999, 100 years after brewing began in the existing building, Princess Anne opened a new visitor centre and museum, housed in the original maltings.

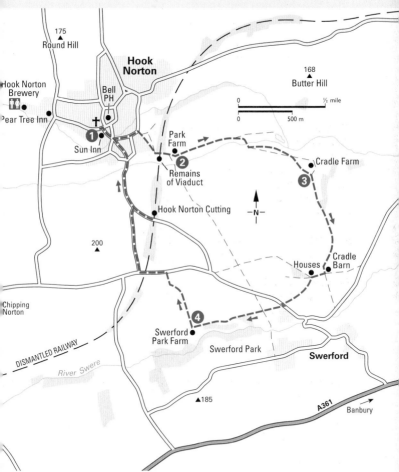

WALK 6 DIRECTIONS

1 With the church on your left, turn right into Middle Hill. Follow it down to the next road and keep ahead over the bridge.

Turn left into Park Road and follow it to the next junction. Continue ahead, keeping a row of bungalows on the left. When the road bends sharp left, join a waymarked bridleway and follow

25

W A L K

6

the track out of Hook Norton. Pass the remains of the railway viaduct and walk to Park Farm.

2 Just before a cattle grid, go through a gate on the left and follow the grassy path to a further gate. Continue along the field-edge to the next gate and follow the obvious track, which soon curves to the right. Cross a ford at the footbridge and make for the next gate. Follow the field boundary and go through a gate into the next field, keeping trees and a hedgerow on the left. Head for a galvanised gate and swing right at the bridleway sign. Walk diagonally across the field and look for a gate in the trees in the top boundary. Follow the grassy path beside the fence to reach a drive.

3 Turn right here, away from Cradle Farm, and walk along to some outbuildings at the point where the drive bends sharp left.

Keep right here and follow the track alongside a pair of semi-detached houses on the right. Emerge from the trees to three tracks; take the middle track up the slope to reach the road. Cross over to a galvanised gate and follow the bridleway between fences, trees and paddocks. On reaching a gate turn right to a wrought-iron gate leading into a field. Turn left and make for a further gate into the next field. Pass to the right-hand side of some fencing and make for a gate in the field boundary.

4 Turn right to join an avenue of lime trees. At length the drive reaches the road. Turn left, then take the first right for Hook Norton. At the first junction, turn right at the sign for Swerford and walk along to the nature reserve at the Hook Norton Cutting. Retrace your steps to the junction and continue ahead towards Hook Norton. Pass the speed restriction sign and keep ahead into the village. Pass Park Road on the right and take Middle Hill back up to the church and the pubs.

The Village of Great Tew – a Rare Plot

Take a stroll through one of Oxfordshire's loveliest villages before exploring undulating countryside to the south.

DISTANCE 4 miles (6.4km)	**MINIMUM TIME** 1hr 45min
ASCENT/GRADIENT 150ft (46m) ▲▲▲	**LEVEL OF DIFFICULTY** ✦✦✦
PATHS Field paths and tracks, stretches of quiet road, 5 stiles	
LANDSCAPE Rolling parkland and farmland on edge of Cotswolds	
SUGGESTED MAP OS Explorer 191 Banbury, Bicester & Chipping Norton	
START/FINISH Grid reference: SP 395294	
DOG FRIENDLINESS Under control across farmland	
PARKING Free car park in Great Tew	
PUBLIC TOILETS None en route	

Arthur Mee, in his book *The King's England – Oxfordshire*, says that 'if our England is a garden, Great Tew is one of its rare plots.' Most would agree. The village is one of the most beautiful in Oxfordshire, a gem of a place that has to be seen to be fully appreciated.

The Fall and Rise of Great Tew

Originally designed as an estate village in the 19th century, with the intention of blending architectural beauty with utility and agricultural management, Great Tew went into decline in later years and virtually became derelict. However, the village has been given a new lease of life, with many of the thatched and ironstone cottages painstakingly restored, and now Great Tew is a designated Conservation Area. The origin of its name is unclear, but Tew is thought to mean 'ridge', of which there are a great many in the area. The village has a fascinating history. In 1036, 53 tenants lived here. By 1276 it had expanded to become a community of at least 75 households. However, the population fell during the 14th century, possibly as a result of the plague.

Falkland's Manor

In later years the village became closely associated with Lucius Carey, 2nd Viscount Falkland. In the 17th century the manor of Great Tew was inherited by the Viscount, a renowned classical scholar, poet and generous host. Falkland later became Secretary of State to Charles I but was killed in 1643 aged 33, serving as an ordinary trooper in the first Battle of Newbury. A later owner, G F Stratton, who inherited Great Tew in 1800, resided in a rather modest late 17th- or early 18th-century house which stood at the southern end of the village. During the early years of the 19th century, Stratton engaged in an ill-fated experiment in estate management, drawing his inspiration from the Scottish agricultural theorist J C Loudon.

The estate subsequently changed hands several times before being acquired by Matthew Robinson Boulton, son of James Watt's partner and

27

one of the giants of the Industrial Revolution, who had a keen eye on its sporting potential. Outlying farms were extensively rebuilt, cottages in the village were re-thatched and other features such as mullioned windows and stone door heads were added. The estate remained the home of the Boulton family for many years. Between 1914 and 1962 Great Tew was administered by trustees on behalf of two unmarried Boulton sisters, but by now the local workforce had decreased and the estate was all but abandoned.

Robb to the Rescue

It was Major Eustace Robb, an old Etonian and descendant of the Boulton family, who moved to the village with the aim of halting its steady decline. His efforts certainly paid off. A stroll through the village today is marked by a conspicuous air of affluence, with coach parties of tourists breaking their journey here to admire one of Oxfordshire's loveliest village attractions.

The noted former political editor John Sergeant spent his childhood at Great Tew. His father was the rector of St Michael's Church during the middle years of the 20th century and Sergeant remembers his time here with great affection. In his memoirs, he describes Great Tew as the ideal place in which to grow up.

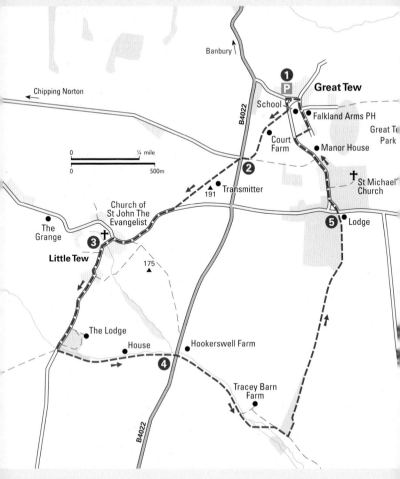

WALK 7 DIRECTIONS

1 From the car park turn left, pass the village turning and take the footpath over a stile on the right, signposted 'Little Tew'. Go diagonally across the field, heading for farm outbuildings on the brow of the hill. Cross a stile in front of silos and continue ahead to a gate and stile. Keep the field boundary on the right, following it to a pair of galvanised gates and a stile leading out to the road at a junction.

2 Cross over and take the path, again signposted to Little Tew. Head diagonally across the field, passing to the right of a transmitter. On reaching the road, turn right and walk down the hill into Little Tew. Pass through the village and turn left at the turning for Enstone. On the corner is the Church of St John the Evangelist.

3 Follow the road out of Little Tew for 0.5 mile (800m) and look for the entrance to The Lodge on the left. Continue downhill to white railings, then turn immediately left at an opening in the hedge leading into a field. Keep along the left boundary and make for a galvanised gate in the field corner. Continue ahead on the grassy path, passing a house over on the left. Keep ahead on the clear track to a kissing gate leading out to the road.

4 Cross over and follow the track signposted to Sandford. Keep alongside trees and where it curves left towards Tracey Barn, keep ahead on the permissive path to a stile. Walk across the field, cross a footbridge, then a stile and turn right to reach a gate by some trees. Continue for a few paces to a gate and waymark on the left. Take the path, keeping a belt of woodland and the field-edge on your left. Beyond the trees, continue ahead into the next field, again beside a tongue of woodland. Pass into the next field and continue alongside trees. Approach a lodge and keep to the left of it.

5 Follow the drive to meet the road, cross over to the junction and take the turning signposted for Great Tew. Pass the entrance to St Michael's Church, which lies peacefully amid the trees of the parkland on the right (see While You're There). Before the school take the fenced path on the right into the village. Turn left at the road and walk past the Falkand Arms, soon to follow the road left back to the car park.

WALK 7

Oxford – Heavenly Jerusalem

*Explore the quiet corners and hidden backwaters
of this beautiful city.*

DISTANCE 2.25 miles (3.6km)	**MINIMUM TIME** 1hr 15min
ASCENT/GRADIENT Negligible ▲▲▲	**LEVEL OF DIFFICULTY** ✦✦✦
PATHS Pavements, field and riverside paths, 4 stiles	
LANDSCAPE Urban, field and meadow on city outskirts	
SUGGESTED MAP OS Explorer 180 Oxford	
START/FINISH Grid reference: SP 513062	
DOG FRIENDLINESS Not much fun in Oxford; under control elsewhere	
PARKING Parking in city centre, or use park-and-ride, or travel by train	
PUBLIC TOILETS Various in Oxford, including Westgate Shopping Centre	

Likened by Thomas Hardy's Jude to 'the heavenly Jerusalem', Oxford's history, beauty and tradition are admired throughout the world, ranking in importance alongside Rome, Athens and Paris. Even when its scholars have moved on, they return time after time to embrace and savour that curiously indefinable 'spirit of Oxford'.

From the top of its highest buildings you begin to realise that Oxford, like Florence, lies at the bottom of a shallow bowl encircled by gentle, protective hills. Originally known as Oxnaforda, Oxford was a settlement of some importance long before the university came into being. It began with the foundation of St Frideswide's nunnery in the 8th century and was first mentioned by name in the Anglo-Saxon Chronicle of 912, which records that King Edward the Elder had made it a fortified frontier position in his defence of Wessex.

The settlement grew and, after the Norman Conquest in 1066, King William appointed his comrade in arms, Robert d'Oilly, to be Oxford's governor. However, it was at the end of the 12th century, when Henry II prevented English clerks from attending the University of Paris, that scholars looked upon Oxford, by then one of the nine most important towns in the country, as somewhere suitable to continue their studies.

Oxford University does not exist as such. Each college is virtually autonomous, with its own rules and administration. It is the treasured and world-famous landmarks that form the real core of the university – in the compact heart of the city you'll find a hugely varied assortment of ancient buildings and monuments, among them the Radcliffe Camera, the Sheldonian Theatre, the Divinity School and the Bodleian Library. Millions of pounds have been spent on restoring and cleaning the stonework of the colleges and university buildings.

A stroll through Oxford's streets reveals much of the city's history, not least its role in the English Civil War. Oxford was the Royalist headquarters as well as the seat of Charles I's parliament. Even Hitler is associated with Oxford. He was so impressed by his interpretation of its tradition that he planned to make it his capital once he had successfully invaded Britain.

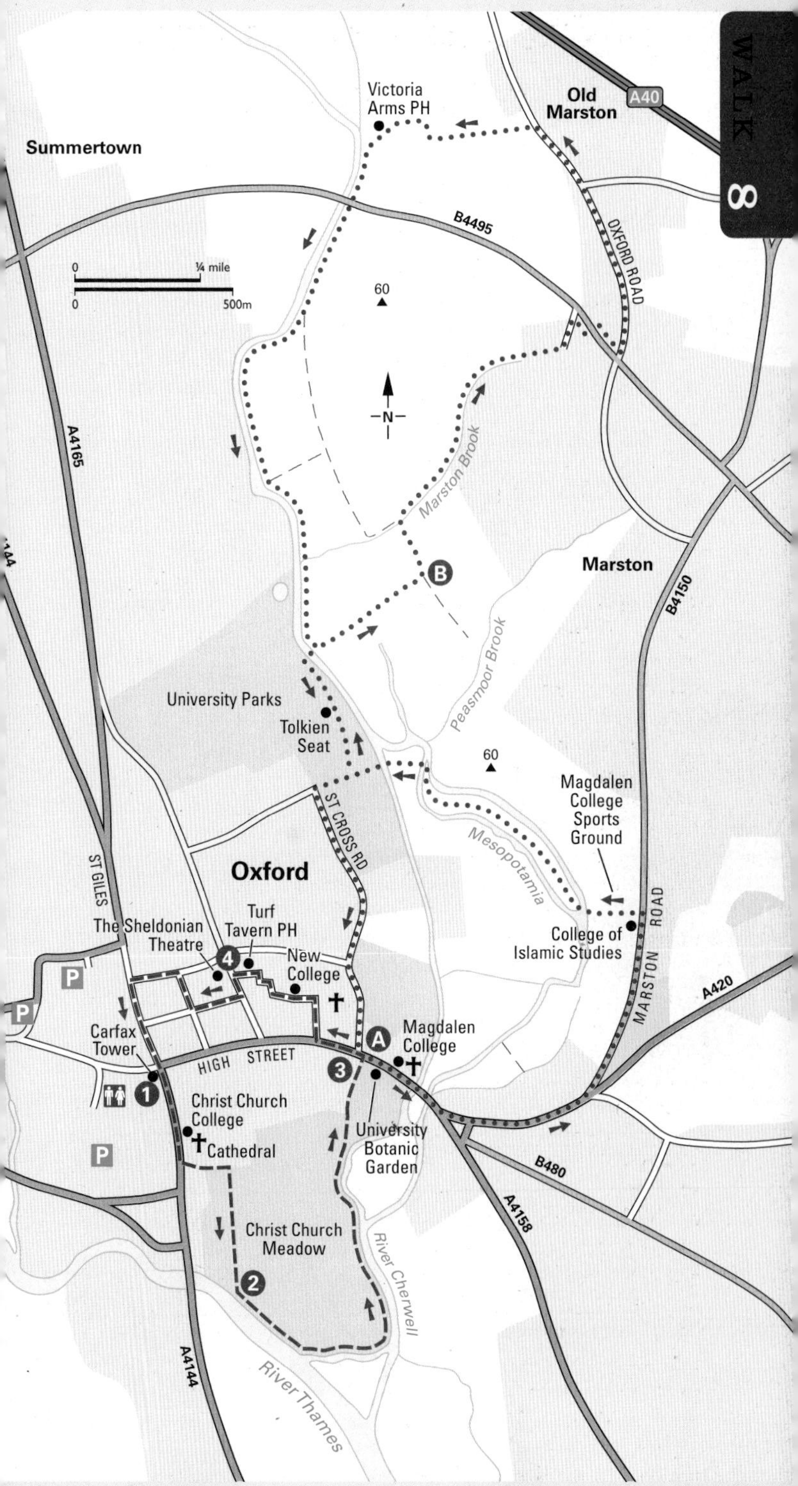

WALK 8

Summertown

Victoria
Arms PH

Old
Marston

A40

B4495

60

Oxford Road

Marston Brook

B

Marston

B4150

Peasmoor Brook

University Parks

Tolkien
Seat

Magdalen
College
Sports
Ground

60

Mesopotamia

Oxford

ST CROSS RD

Turf
Tavern PH

The Sheldonian
Theatre

4

New
College

Carfax
Tower

College of
Islamic Studies

MARSTON ROAD

A420

A

Magdalen
College

3

HIGH   STREET

1

University
Botanic
Garden

Christ Church
College

Cathedral

Christ Church
Meadow

B480

A4158

2

River Cherwell

St Giles

A4165

A4144

River Thames

A4144

0   ¼ mile
0   500m

—N—

WALK 8

WALK 8 DIRECTIONS

1 Start at the Carfax, where four streets converge – Carfax comes from the Latin *quadrifurcus*, for 'four-forked'. Carfax Tower is where Charles II was proclaimed King in 1660. Walk ahead into St Aldates and head for the visitor entrance to Christ Church, Oxford's largest college, founded in 1525 by Cardinal Wolsey. When he was disgraced it was refounded as King Henry VIII's College. It became known as Christ Church when the college and the cathedral became one. Christ Church has had many notable students, including three Prime Ministers – Robert Peel, William Gladstone and Lord Salisbury. John Wesley, Lewis Carroll and W H Auden also studied here. The steeple is believed to be the first ever built in this country. At the visitor entrance to Christ Church turn right and walk down the tree-lined New Walk. On the left is the green expanse of Christ Church Meadow.

WHERE TO EAT AND DRINK

There are many pubs, tea rooms and restaurants in and around Oxford. The Turf Tavern, off New College Lane near the Bridge of Sighs, has plenty of choice and a cosy, welcoming atmosphere.

2 On reaching the Thames tow path, swing left and follow the riverbank. Keep ahead until you reach the confluence of the Thames and the River Cherwell. There is a steeply arched footbridge here. Avoid it and keep alongside the Cherwell. The river meanders between the meadows and sports fields. Leave the river bank and pass through wrought-iron gates to walk up Rose Lane.

3 With Magdalen Bridge and Magdalen College bell tower on your right, turn left at the High Street or 'the High', as it is known in Oxford. Cross Longwall Street and turn right into Queen's Lane. The high perimeter wall of Queen's College is on the left and on the right are St Edmund Hall and the former parish church of St Peter-in-the-East. Continue into New College Lane and on the right, beyond the arch, is the entrance to New College. Keep along New College Lane to the Bridge of Sighs, a 1913 replica of its Venice namesake, and in front of you is the Sheldonian Theatre.

4 Designed by Sir Christopher Wren and completed in 1669, the theatre was built to hold important university meetings and ceremonies. Turn left here for the Radcliffe Camera and cross Radcliffe Square towards Brasenose College, which probably took its name from a brazen door-knocker in the shape of a nose. Turn right into Brasenose Lane, then right again into Turl Street, cutting between Jesus College and Exeter College. Make for Broad Street and on the right is St Giles, where Charles I drilled his men during the Civil War. Turn left into Cornmarket Street, passing the Church of St Michael at the North Gate. Its Saxon tower is the oldest building in Oxford and originally linked the city wall and the North Gate. Return to the Carfax.

WHAT TO LOOK OUT FOR

Alongside Rose Lane, the University Botanic Garden, established in 1621 by the Earl of Danby, is Britain's oldest botanic garden. The 8,000 species of plants demonstrate the plant kingdom's enormous diversity.

On to Mesopotamia

*Escape the bustle of the city streets and follow the
River Cherwell to Marston.*

See map and information panel for Walk 8

DISTANCE *7 miles (11.3km)*   **MINIMUM TIME** *3hrs*

ASCENT/GRADIENT *Negligible* ▲▲▲   **LEVEL OF DIFFICULTY** ✚✚✚

WALK 9 DIRECTIONS
(Walk 8 option)

On reaching the High Street, turn right towards Magdalen Bridge, Point **Ⓐ**. Cross it and follow St Clements Street. Walk along to London Place, then branch left into Marston Road. Follow the road to Magdalen College Sports Ground and turn left just before it, taking a metalled path down to the River Cherwell. Follow the path to a strip of land, between the river and a mill stream, known as Mesopotamia, from the Greek for 'between rivers'.

Turn left over a bridge, then swing right on the opposite bank to enter the University Parks. Turn left and follow a concrete path, cross a bridge and turn immediately right at a kissing gate. Fork right, keep alongside the Cherwell and make for the Tolkien seat, in memory of J R R Tolkien, Professor of Anglo-Saxon at Merton College between 1925 and 1945. Cross the next bridge, following the path ahead.

Turn left at the next junction, Point **Ⓑ**, and then right at the next, avoiding a footbridge here. Cross a footbridge and stile and turn right, skirting a field to enter woodland. Go through a kissing gate and eventually the path reaches the entrance to Marston Middle School. Follow the drive and swing left just beyond the primary school. Turn right after a few paces, passing through the subway. Follow the walkway to the right, then turn left at Oxford Road.

Walk through Old Marston, veer left into Mill Lane and turn left for the Victoria Arms. Make for the far corner of the car park and follow the woodland path beside the river. Cross the B4495 and continue on the footpath. On reaching two stiles, side by side, take the right path and keep to the riverside path, passing Wolfson College.

Cross the river at the bridge crossed earlier and turn left, passing the Tolkien seat. Walk through the Parks, keep right at the fork and follow the path as it sweeps to the right to reach a map of University Parks. Turn left here, pass Linacre College and continue ahead along St Cross Road. Pass Holywell Street and follow Longwall Street, passing the garage where William Morris (1887–1963) built the prototype for the 'bullnose' Morris Oxford. Walk along to the High Street, turn right and rejoin Walk 8 at Point **❸**.

Godstow's Tale of Jealousy

Take a walk across ancient grazing land to Britain's greatest river.

DISTANCE 4.5 miles (7.2km)   MINIMUM TIME 1hr 45min

ASCENT/GRADIENT Negligible ▲▲▲   LEVEL OF DIFFICULTY ✦✦✦

PATHS Meadow paths and tracks, tow path, road (can be busy)

LANDSCAPE Ancient grazing land north-west of Oxford city

SUGGESTED MAP OS Explorer 180 Oxford

START / FINISH Grid reference: SP 487094

DOG FRIENDLINESS Under control on Port Meadow – on lead if cattle about

PARKING Public car park (free) at Lower Wolvercote

PUBLIC TOILETS At car park

WALK 10 DIRECTIONS

From the car park keep right and walk through Lower Wolvercote. Pass between the houses and on to the Red Lion and the White Hart. Pass Home Close and Rowland Close, followed by the local post office. Continue to Elmthorpe Road and at this point turn right, passing through the gate to reach Wolvercote Common. Approach the railway and, 50yds (46m) before it, swing slightly right, following a grassy path out towards Port Meadow. The path gradually curves away from the line, heading for a cobbled bridge over a ditch.

WHERE TO EAT AND DRINK

Wolvercote has a number of pubs, most serving a range of traditional food and drink. The Perch at Binsey and the Thames-side Trout at Godstow both have a wide choice of dishes.

Maintain the same direction across this breezy, open ground and look for barges and sailing boats gliding along the distant Thames. Look for and go through a kissing gate over to the left. Keep right at the junction beyond it and right again at the next track. Head south through Burgess Field Nature Park to rejoin the open ground and follow a concrete track along the edge of Port Meadow.

Head towards a car park and turn right just before it at a kissing gate. Follow the bridleway to a wide footbridge over the Thames, turn right to a second footbridge and cross to the opposite bank, heading upstream now beside Bossom's Boatyard and Medley Sailing Club. Continue on the Thames Path, passing a turning to the Perch at Binsey, and on to Godstow Lock. Ahead are the remains of Godstow Abbey where, according to legend, the body of Fair Rosamond, the beautiful mistress of Henry II, was buried after she had been murdered by a jealous queen.

All that is left of Godstow Abbey is a walled enclosure with, in one corner, the shell of a 16th-century chapel. The abbey was founded in 1139, and the nunnery here was where Rosamond de Clifford was sent by her father to finish her education. But fate took a hand. Henry II spotted Rosamond one day after she had been picked to work in a high-class brothel – now the famous Trout Inn, one of Oxfordshire's most famous pubs.

WHILE YOU'RE THERE

Covering 345 acres (140ha), the ancient common of Port Meadow is where the Freemen and Commoners of Oxford can graze geese, horses and cattle. The grazing arrangements were mentioned in the Domesday survey of 1086.

Henry was so taken with Rosamond that he installed her as his mistress in his royal palace at Woodstock, where Blenheim Palace now stands (see Walk 21). She even bore him two sons – William Longspee, Earl of Salisbury, and Geoffrey who became Lord Chancellor of England. The house was secret, surrounded by a maze to protect Rosamond from Henry's queen, the formidable Eleanor of Aquitaine. However, Eleanor discovered what was going on and set about getting rid of Rosamond. She managed to penetrate the maze, which was shaped like a knot, and poisoned the woman who had become a rival for her husband's affections.

Or did she? Tradition has it that Rosamond was murdered but it's possible that she escaped death and retired to Godstow to become a nun, before dying, probably from natural causes, in 1176. Her tomb was found there. As for Eleanor, she was an extremely unpopular queen and there were many people who were eager to see her discredited.

After Rosamond's death, royal endowments paid for silk curtains draped around the tomb and there were continuous prayers for her soul. But Bishop Hugh of Lincoln rejected such indulgence and ordered her remains to be removed. However, on his departure, the nuns concealed the bones in a perfumed leather bag, depositing them in a lead coffin in the Chapter House. Years later, the famous antiquarian John Leland recorded that when the coffin was opened, it was found to have a sweet smell.

The nunnery was eventually dissolved in the mid-16th century, passing into the hands of George Owen, Henry VIII's physician. In the Civil War it was garrisoned for Charles I but seized in 1646 and almost completely destroyed by order of the Puritan commander, Colonel Fairfax. Little remains of the place now, but with a little imagination you can picture a young girl who enthralled an adulterous king, walking by the placid waters of the Thames.

WHAT TO LOOK OUT FOR

As you return to the car park look for a memorial on the wall by the road to two members of the Royal Flying Corps. They met their deaths in a monoplane crash just to the north of this site in September 1912. The stone was erected as a tribute to the bravery of these two British officers.

Continue ahead, keeping to the right of the ruins to the road. Turn right here and pass the famous Trout Inn before returning to the car park.

Myths of the Rollright Stones

*From Chipping Norton to an ancient site
associated with a charming legend.*

DISTANCE 8 miles (12.9km)   **MINIMUM TIME** 4hrs

ASCENT/GRADIENT 295ft (90m) ▲▲▲   **LEVEL OF DIFFICULTY** +++

PATHS Field paths and tracks, country roads, 7 stiles

LANDSCAPE Rolling hills on the Oxfordshire/Warwickshire border

SUGGESTED MAP OS Explorer 191 Banbury, Bicester
& Chipping Norton

START / FINISH Grid reference: SP 313271

DOG FRIENDLINESS Under control or on lead across farmland, one lengthy
stretch of country road and busy streets in Chipping Norton

PARKING Free car park off A44, in centre of Chipping Norton

PUBLIC TOILETS At car park

Commanding a splendid position overlooking the hills and valleys of the north-east Cotswolds, the Rollright Stones comprise the Whispering Knights, the King's Men and the King Stone. These intriguing stones are steeped in myth and legend.

Mystical Theories

It seems a king was leading his army in this quiet corner of Oxfordshire while five of his knights stood together conspiring against him. The king met a witch near by who told him he would be King of England if he could see the settlement of Long Compton in seven long strides. As he approached the top of the ridge a mound of earth suddenly rose up before him, preventing him from seeing the village and so the king, his soldiers and his knights were all turned to stone.

In reality the Rollright Stones form a group of prehistoric megalithic monuments created from large natural boulders found within about 600yds (549m) of the site. The stones are naturally pitted, giving them astonishing and highly unusual shapes. The five Whispering Knights are the remains of a Portal Dolmen burial chamber, probably from 3800–3000 BC, long before the stone circle. It would have been imposing in its day and it is the easternmost burial chamber of this kind in Britain. The King Stone stands apart from the others. The 8ft (2.4m) tall single standing stone was almost certainly erected to mark the site of a Bronze Age cemetery which was in use around 1800–1500 BC.

Finally, you come to the King's Men Stone Circle – a ceremonial monument thought to have been built around 2500–2000 BC. There are over 70 stones here. Originally there were about 105 stones forming a continuous wall except for one narrow entrance. The King's Men Stones are arranged in an unditched circle about 100ft (30m) across and ranging in size from just a few inches to 7ft (2m). Here and there the stones are so close they almost touch.

CHIPPING NORTON

It is not clear what the stone circle was used for but it may well have had some significance in religious and secular ceremonies. Most mysterious of all is why this particular site was chosen. Visitors to the Rollright Stones have questioned their origin but they remain a mystery.

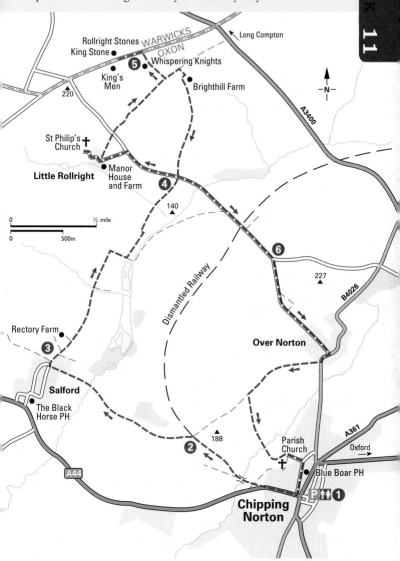

WALK 11 DIRECTIONS

❶ Follow the A44, New Street, downhill. Pass Penhurst School, then veer right through a kissing gate. Skirt the left-hand edge of the recreation ground and aim for a gate. Descend to a bridge and, when the path forks, keep right. Go up the slope to a kissing gate. Cross a drive and continue to the next tarmac drive. Keep ahead to a stile and along the right-hand edge of a field. Make for gate and drop down to some double gates on the right.

WHERE TO EAT AND DRINK

Chipping Norton offers a variety of pubs, hotels and tea rooms. Try the rambling old Blue Boar with its views of the Market Place and the town's many historic buildings. Here you'll find a good choice of dishes, including Gloucestershire sausages and baked rabbit. The Black Horse at Salford offers the chance to stop off for refreshment during the walk.

2 Go through. Turn sharp left and walk towards Salford, keeping the hedge on the left. Continue into the village and soon turn right by some grass and a sign, 'Trout Lakes – Rectory Farm'.

3 Follow the track to a right-hand bend. Go straight ahead here, following the field-edge. Make for a gate ahead and turn right in the next field. About 100yds (91m) before the field corner, turn left and follow the path across to an opening in the boundary. Veer left, then immediately right to skirt the field. Cross a little stream and maintain your direction in the next field to reach the road.

WHILE YOU'RE THERE

Have a look at Chipping Norton, or 'Chippy' as the locals call it. One of the gateways to the Cotswolds, the town prospered as a result of the wool trade. The church, though not prominently placed in the town, is impressive.

4 Turn left, then left again for Little Rollright. After visiting the church, retrace your steps to the D'Arcy Dalton Way on the left. Follow the path up the field slope to the road. Cross over and continue on the way between fields. Head for some trees and approach a stile.

Don't cross it; instead, turn left and skirt the field, passing close to the Whispering Knights.

5 On reaching the road, turn left and visit the site of the Rollright Stones. Return to the Whispering Knights, head down the field to the stile and cross it to an immediate second stile. Walk ahead along a grassy path and turn right at the next stile towards Brighthill Farm. Pass alongside the buildings to a stile, head diagonally right down the field to a double stile, keep the boundary on your right and head for a galvanised gate in the bottom right corner of the field. Make for the bottom right corner of the next field, go through a gate and skirt the field, turning left at the road.

WHAT TO LOOK OUT FOR

The manor house at Little Rollright was once important. It was the home of William Blower who gave St Philip's Church its pinnacled tower in 1617. The church, which dates mostly from the 15th century, has two 17th-century monuments to the local Dixon and Blower families.

6 Keep right at the next fork and head towards the village of Over Norton. Walk through the village to the T-junction. Turn right and when the road swings to the left by Cleeves Corner, join a track signposted 'Salford'. When the hedges on the left give way, look for a waymark on the left. Follow the path down the slope, make for two kissing gates and then follow the path alongside a stone wall to reach the parish church. Join Church Lane and follow it as far as the T-junction. Turn right and return to the town centre.

Adlestrop to Chastleton

From a timeless village to an age-old house.

DISTANCE 4 miles (6.4km)	MINIMUM TIME 2hrs
ASCENT/GRADIENT 427ft (130m) ▲▲▲	LEVEL OF DIFFICULTY +++
PATHS *Meadows, lanes, woodland, 7 stiles*	
LANDSCAPE *Low rolling hills north of Chipping Norton*	
SUGGESTED MAP *OS Explorer OL45 The Cotswolds*	
START/FINISH *Grid reference: SP 241271*	
DOG FRIENDLINESS *Under control across farmland; some road walking*	
PARKING *Car park (donations) beside village hall, Adlestrop*	
PUBLIC TOILETS *None en route*	

The walk starts in the sleepy village of Adlestrop. It was not always so quiet, for trains used to stop here. The poet Edward Thomas (1878–1917) wrote a wistful little verse in which he recalled stopping here unexpectedly on the express train, apparently in the middle of nowhere, and listening to the birdsong. Set in deep, lush countryside, Adlestrop still feels well off the beaten track. Its houses are a pleasing harmony of old and new, stone roofs alternating with thatch, and cottage gardens to die for.

Chastleton House

One of the finest Jacobean mansions in England, Chastleton House stands on the hillside above its village, aloof and self-contained. The house has a magical stillness about it. It was built between 1603 and 1618 by a local wool merchant, Walter Jones, on land purchased from Robert Catesby, one of the Gunpowder plotters. Unusually, the house was to be occupied for the next 400 years by the same family.

Time-worn Perfection

The handsome grey-stone frontage of the house, with its tall windows and symmetrical gables and staircase towers, can be seen clearly from the road. If you want to see inside, however, you are urged to book ahead, as opening hours and numbers are strictly limited. Chastleton is no grand showplace and, since its acquisition, the National Trust has been careful to conserve the house in its peaceful, time-worn perfection, rather than attempt to restore it to some former glory. There is a panelled hall and an ornate great chamber and, on the top floor, a vast long gallery with plastered ceiling looks out over the gardens. Much of the furniture is original and the chambers are richly adorned with embroideries, quilts and tapestries.

Chastleton may have led a quiet life, but hardly a dull one. A secret room above the parlour was used to hide a fugitive in the Civil War. Arthur Jones was a Royalist, and had fought for the King – and lost – at the Battle of Worcester in 1651. He fled to his father's house at Chastleton and was forced into the hiding place when a party of soldiers arrived in hot pursuit. Arthur's wife, Sarah, was obliged to put them up for the night. This resourceful woman laced their ale with laudanum and, while his pursuers snored, Arthur made his escape.

Croquet on the Lawn

The formal gardens at Chastleton are contemporary with the house, its lawns studded with dark topiary. It is sometimes claimed that croquet was invented here. In fact, the game had been around for centuries, but was only introduced to England in 1852. The rules of the game were set out for the first time here at Chastleton in 1865.

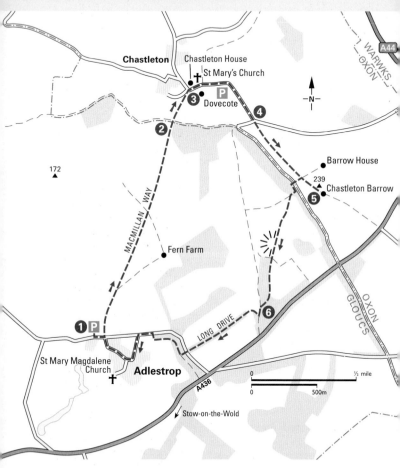

WALK 12 DIRECTIONS

1 Turn left on to the road and left again up a broad track, signposted 'Macmillan Way'. Pass a barn and continue to a stile by a gate and enter a meadow. Bear left by a yellow waymarker. Walk along the bottom of the field, with

Fern Farm up to your right. Cross a stile in the top left corner and continue up the fence. Soon cross a stile to your left and continue up the same line, passing a bulging oak tree on your right. Cross another stile and continue straight ahead up the field. The hill gets steeper.

❷ Cross a stile by a wooden gate and walk up through the line of trees. Continue straight across the next field. Go over the crest of the hill and through an iron gate, into the Chastleton Estate. Continue straight ahead up an avenue of trees. Go through two gates to reach the road.

WHAT TO LOOK OUT FOR

Walking into the green ring of Chastleton Barrow is an eerie experience. Surrounded by a bank or rampart planted with trees, it clearly functioned once as a defensive site, probably in the Iron Age. A track linked the camp with the Rollright Stones (see Walk 11). This wide grassy amphitheatre on the hilltop is now used to hold cattle.

❸ Turn right and walk along the road, passing Chastleton House on your left, then St Mary's Church. Pass the arcaded dovecote on the right. Stay on the road, which bends up right, and pass a car park on your right.

❹ Where the road bends sharply right, turn left into a private road. Cross a cattle grid and immediately turn right. Go through a gate and take the bridleway diagonally left up the field, parallel with the road. On a level with Barrow House farm, go through a small gate, cross the drive and take the left of two gates opposite. Go through two more gates to enter the tree circle of Chastleton Barrow.

❺ When you have seen the barrow, retrace your route to the drive and turn left. At the road cross over and go through a gate. Turn left after a few paces and walk through the trees to enter a field. Follow the path diagonally right across the field, with views

WHILE YOU'RE THERE

The walk offers excellent views across to the busy market town of Stow-on-the-Wold, reached along the A436. Perched on the very edge of the Wolds, it is known to catch any blast of wind, and can be icy in winter – hence the local saying, 'Stow-on-the-Wold, where the wind blows cold.' This is antique-hunter's heaven, however, and there's a steady flow of visitors.

to Stow-on-the-Wold. Keep straight on down, passing some barns to your left. Cross a track and walk ahead down the edge of woodland. At the bottom corner bear right into the woods. Follow the winding path and emerge at a field.

❻ Turn left along the track. Turn right before you reach the gateway, and walk down the edge of the field. Go through a gate into the Long Drive. Follow this path through the trees and emerge on to the road. Cross, go through a gateway on the other side and soon turn right along a narrow footpath. Follow this through the trees; cross a stile and turn left along the road. Take the first turning left and walk through Adlestrop village, keeping right to return to the start of the walk.

WHERE TO EAT AND DRINK

The venerable villages of Lower Oddington and Upper Oddington offer an appealing diversion on your way to Stow-on-the-Wold and are served by two good pubs. The Fox at Lower Oddington is opposite a beautiful little manor house. Continue through the villages to reach the Horse and Groom at Upper Oddington, which describes itself as a village inn and has the bonus of a big car park behind.

A Right Royal Scandal at Cumnor Place

Explore the countryside surrounding a village that is the setting for a centuries-old mystery.

DISTANCE 5.5 miles (8.8km)   MINIMUM TIME 2hrs 30min

ASCENT/GRADIENT 164ft (50m) ▲▲▲   LEVEL OF DIFFICULTY +++

PATHS Field paths, quiet lanes and tracks, 1 stile

LANDSCAPE Fields and pasture adjacent to River Thames

SUGGESTED MAP OS Explorer 180 Oxford

START/FINISH Grid reference: SP 458044

DOG FRIENDLINESS On lead in villages and on country lanes

PARKING Spaces by village hall in Cumnor

PUBLIC TOILETS None en route

Sadly, a stone fireplace set in a bank in an Oxfordshire churchyard is virtually all that is left of Cumnor Place, the setting for a mystery that has baffled historians for centuries. The manor of Cumnor was once owned by Abingdon Abbey and the remains of the house, the abbot's summer residence, form part of the extended parish churchyard. Cumnor Place, which stood to the west of the church, was demolished in 1810 by the Earl of Abingdon.

So what exactly happened here so long ago? What was it that scandalised the country? Following the Dissolution, the house was leased by Anthony Forster, the steward of Lord Robert Dudley, Queen Elizabeth's favourite.

The Tale of Dudley and Amy

Dudley, third son of the Earl of Warwick, married Amy Robsart in 1550. She was the only daughter of a wealthy Norfolk landowner and it seems likely the couple met when Dudley travelled with his father to East Anglia to quell a local rebellion. Amy was young when she married, only 18, but the couple seemed happy together – at least on the face of it. However, three years later Dudley found himself in the Tower of London, charged with conspiring to prevent Mary Tudor from getting her inheritance. He was later pardoned and resumed life on his father-in-law's estates in Norfolk.

A Change of Circumstances

The death of Mary in 1558 and the accession of Elizabeth to the throne had a significant impact on Dudley. He and the new Queen had been friends since childhood and now they had the opportunity to become even closer. Elizabeth was certainly smitten – it is said she smiled on no-one as she smiled on Dudley.

While her husband spent much of his time away at court, Amy stayed with friends in the country. She was lonely without him and there were rumours that she was ailing. Whispers of Dudley's close friendship with the Queen would not have helped matters.

CUMNOR

In 1560 Lady Dudley went to stay with Anthony Forster and his wife at Cumnor Place. On Sunday 8 September she died after falling downstairs and breaking her neck. On hearing the news at court, Dudley allegedly showed no outward signs of grief or distress, perhaps fearing that the circumstances surrounding his wife's death would damage his reputation. The main question was 'what caused her death?' Was it suicide, natural causes, a tragic accident or, worst of all, murder? If so, did Dudley plan it and was Forster involved? He knew that if Dudley were free to marry the Queen, then his own future would be assured.

Nothing was proved. The matter was investigated fully and the jury returned a verdict of 'mischance or accidental death'. But was it? Within three years of Amy's death the Queen made him Earl of Leicester.

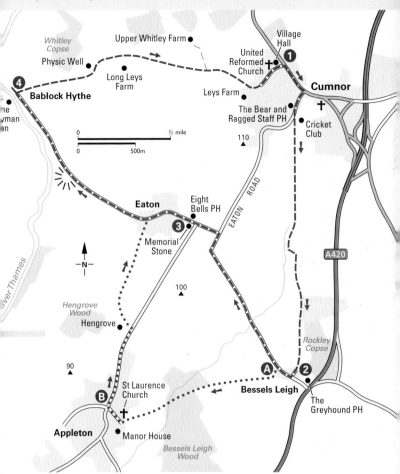

WALK 13 DIRECTIONS

1 Turn right from the parking area and walk along to the mini-roundabout. Turn right into Appleton Road and pass the Bear and Ragged Staff pub on the right. Veer half left just a few paces beyond it and join a footpath signposted to Bessels Leigh. Pass the cricket club on the left and continue on the track.

When it peters out continue ahead in the field, keeping a ditch on your right. Pass alongside a line of trees on the far side of the field, turn left, then turn right and make for an opening in the corner, concealed by vegetation in summer. Go straight on to a galvanised gate and keep some houses over to the left beyond the pasture. Cross a footbridge to a galvanised gate, swing left and follow the path beside a fence, keeping in line with the telephone wires, and make for a gate in the field corner. Follow the drive to the road.

❷ To visit The Greyhound pub, turn left. To continue the walk turn right and follow the road through Bessels Leigh and continue out in the countryside, cutting between farmland. On reaching a junction, keep left to the next junction. Go straight on into the village of Eaton and pass the Eight Bells pub.

❸ Follow the lane out of Eaton and through flat countryside.

When it becomes enclosed by trees, look for a view of the Thames on the left. Continue to Bablock Hythe and look across the river to the Ferryman Inn. Walk back along the lane for a few paces and turn left at the bridleway signposted 'Cumnor'.

❹ Pass through a gate and follow the enclosed path (can be wet and muddy in winter) gently uphill and when, some time later, the path curves to the right, look for the Physic Well in the trees to the left of your route. This is a muddy spring which was once greatly valued as a source of healing waters. Emerge from the trees and cut between fields towards pylons. Go through a gate, join a drive and walk ahead. Ignore the turning to Upper Whitley Farm and continue into Cumnor, passing Leys Farm on the right. Look for the United Reformed Church and return to the village hall.

A Woodland Detour to Appleton

Extend the walk to look at a classic brick and stone village.
See map and information panel for Walk 13

DISTANCE 6.5 miles (10.5km) **MINIMUM TIME** 2hrs 45min

ASCENT/GRADIENT *Negligible* ▲▲▲ **LEVEL OF DIFFICULTY** ✦✦✦

WALK 14 DIRECTIONS
(Walk 13 option)

Turn left at the sign for Appleton and go through the galvanised gate, Point **Ⓐ**. Follow the track/road to the right and straight along to two sets of galvanised gates and some farm outbuildings on the right. Continue across the pasture to a kissing gate leading into Bessels Leigh Wood and keep ahead alongside the fence.

This area has been continuously wooded for over 400 years but has recently been altered by a process of partial planting of non-native species. These days, the woodland is managed for quiet recreation and wildlife, and the timber growth will be managed to take full advantage of this resource for the future. Birch and oak are among the trees to be found here, while sycamore is the result of planting in the 1950s. Roe, fallow and muntjac deer are known to inhabit the woods.

Pass a stile and footpath on the right and continue ahead through the wood. Emerging from the trees, cut across a footbridge and follow a straight path between fences and pastures. Go through two gates and across a footbridge and approach Appleton church. Pass to the side of it to the drive and follow it into the village.

Follow Church Road to the T-junction and turn right opposite the post office, Point **Ⓑ**.

Appleton is a picturesque village of brick and stone houses. The manor house is partly 12th-century, one of the oldest in the county, and its Norman doorway is still visible over the churchyard wall. The church is essentially Norman with a 15th-century tower and some later additions. Inside is a tomb to a lord of the manor, a member of the Fettiplace family, who was knighted by Queen Elizabeth when she visited Woodstock.

Head out of Appleton, passing the village sign. Just a few paces beyond the entrance to a house, turn left at a footpath sign for Eaton. Follow the track as it sweeps to the right and skirts the field, keeping alongside the boundary. Join a clear track on a bend and continue ahead. Pass some farm outbuildings to reach the road at Eaton, rejoining Walk 13 at this point.

Overleaf: A woodland path winds through an autumnal beech wood (Walk 15)

Stonesfield Slate Sculpting

*Find out what a pretty village has in common
with Oxford's colleges.*

DISTANCE 3.5 miles (5.7km) MINIMUM TIME 1hr 30min
ASCENT/GRADIENT 164ft (50m) ▲▲▲ LEVEL OF DIFFICULTY ✚✚✚
PATHS Riverside path, tracks and roads (can be busy)
LANDSCAPE Undulating country bisected by River Evenlode
SUGGESTED MAP OS Explorer 180 Oxford
START/FINISH Grid reference: SP 393171
DOG FRIENDLINESS On lead in Stonesfield and along road on return leg
PARKING Spaces in village centre
PUBLIC TOILETS None en route

WALK 15 DIRECTIONS

Stonesfield is a hilly village closely associated with the tradition of slate mining. The stone is a type of Jurassic limestone known as 'pendle'. It's a little-known fact outside Oxfordshire, but many of the stone roofing slates used in this part of the county come from Stonesfield, as do the slates of many Oxford colleges. The slate was reputedly the best, lightest and least porous of roofing materials, with the local stone pits and slate quarries dating mainly from the 16th century.

The village is known for a charming winter-time tradition

dating back to when slate mining was the main industry in the area. When a sharp frost was expected, the church bells would toll, often in the middle of the night, reminding the residents of Stonesfield of the need to ensure that the stone was immediately uncovered and exposed to the elements. This was not part of some bizzare rural custom. There was method in their madness.

When the villagers rose from their beds in the morning, they would discover that the freezing temperature had split the stone neatly into layers which could then be sculpted into slates. The Romans, who constructed several villas near Stonesfield during their occupation, probably quarried stone in the district. The village has expanded hugely over the years but the centre of Stonesfield, in the vicinity of the church, still has a charm and character, retaining a hint of the past.

The last pit at Stonesfield closed before the First World War, and the last slate miner died in the

WHAT TO LOOK OUT FOR

Parts of this walk in the Evenlode Valley are a sheer delight, especially where the route crosses the Evenlode, described by Hilaire Belloc – an energetic walker, writer and politician, who attended Balliol College, Oxford – as 'a lovely river, all alone… forgotten in the western wolds.'

STONESFIELD

1940s. Today, the inhabitants of the village earn their living in other ways, many of them working in nearby Oxford. Demand for replacement slates is now met using materials from demolished buildings.

With the church over to the right, leave Stonesfield by heading south. Pass rows of houses and, when the road turns sharp right at Churchfields, go straight on into Brook Lane. Follow the unmade road, pass a turning to the Rectory on the right and lines of bungalows on the left and continue down towards the River Evenlode. Ahead of you are glimpses of a rolling, wooded landscape in the valley. Descend a series of steps, following the sunken path to the river bank.

WHERE TO EAT AND DRINK

Contemporary mixes well with the traditional at the civilised White Horse, which offers Hooky on tap and innovative dishes on seasonal menus in the quirky chic bar and cosy restaurant. Secluded front garden for summer alfresco eating and drinking.

Cross the river via the footbridge and keep heading south, following the bridleway across the fields. The Evenlode can be seen over to the right, snaking through the countryside. Pass through a gate and then turn immediately right to follow a waymarked path alongside the river. The walk cuts through margins of vegetation and undergrowth before the outline of a railway bridge looms into view ahead. Pass under the bridge and follow the path as it runs close to the water's edge. In places, the boughs of the trees reach down to touch the surface of the Evenlode.

Beech trees line the bank along here, and soon the river sweeps away to the right.

On reaching the road, walk along to the junction and turn right for Stonesfield. Cross the Evenlode and pass some roadside dwellings. Pass over the railway line, then turn immediately left for Fawler and Charlbury. Follow this road for about 0.5 mile (800m). Further on, a curtain of woodland can be seen in the distance, draped spectacularly across the valley – one of many scenic highlights on this walk.

Turn right by a cottage and head up the track towards the stone outbuildings of Oaklands Farm. Keep right at the buildings, following the track round the east side of the farm. Head north on the track, across open country, with views of Stonesfield in the distance. The track bends right before passing a copper beech tree. Soon you reach the road.

Turn left and then right by some stone barns and industrial units. Continue along the lane into Stonesfield, keeping right at the next junction. In a few paces take the arrowed footpath right and follow the narrow metalled path uphill between cottages to a road opposite the Methodist church. Turn right and walk along High Street. Soon you reach the church where the walk began.

WHILE YOU'RE THERE

Visit the fully excavated North Leigh Roman Villa, a short drive to the south of Stonesfield. The site is close to the Evenlode and is a fine example of a Roman villa with a good mosaic pavement. The Roman road, Akeman Street, crosses the river here.

Churchill
and Cornwell

A walk linking two intriguing villages
on the D'Arcy Dalton Way.

DISTANCE 5.5 miles (8.8km)   **MINIMUM TIME** 2hrs 30min

ASCENT/GRADIENT 459ft (140m) ▲▲▲   **LEVEL OF DIFFICULTY** ✦✦✦

PATHS Open farmland, village lanes, quiet roads, 5 stiles

LANDSCAPE Broad, open valley once used by a railway line

SUGGESTED MAP OS Explorer OL45 The Cotswolds

START / FINISH Grid reference: SP 270271

DOG FRIENDLINESS Some road walking, otherwise good

PARKING Lay-by beside phone box at Cornwell

PUBLIC TOILETS None en route

There's a slightly theatrical air about Cornwell. It huddles on one side of a small valley, smugly holding on to its secrets, for, as part of the Cornwell Manor Estate, it is private and inaccessible. You may look, but not touch. The manor itself, where owner Peter Ward and his family live today, is carefully screened from prying eyes, except for the lovely stone front, which boldly faces up to the road from behind its high wrought iron gate.

Cornwell

Cornwell's best-known secret is that it was thoroughly remodelled just before the Second World War by Clough Williams-Ellis (1883–1978). Born in Northamptonshire, Williams-Ellis developed an eclectic design style that mixed architectural details in a particularly flamboyant way. By the time he was working on Cornwell, his own pet project at Portmeirion in North Wales – what he called his home for fallen buildings – was already well established. The then owner of Cornwell, Mrs Anthony Gillson, employed Williams-Ellis to modernise the village, but also to create the magnificent terraced gardens at the manor, along with building alterations. His influence may be clearly seen on the village hall (originally the school), with its bowed end and eccentric chimney stack-cum-bellcote.

The little Church of St Peter remained untouched at this time, though the handsome wooden candelabras are attributed to the style of Clough Williams-Ellis. It dates from Norman times, and it is believed that a village once surrounded the church, but disappeared during the plague years.

Churchill

In direct contrast to Cornwell, Churchill's attractions are up-front and open to view. The tower of All Saints' Church dominates the skyline for miles around, and if it looks familiar, that's because it's a scaled-down model of the tower of Magdalene College, Oxford. As the choristers of that famous establishment sing from their tower to greet the dawn on May Day, so local choristers gather at the top of All Saints' to do the same. The church was built in 1826 by James Langston, a mover and shaker in the village, and it is he who is affectionately remembered with the large and elaborate fountain next door.

Churchill boasts two famous sons. The first is Warren Hastings (1732–1818), a colourful figure who rose to become Governor-General of India, and lost his fortune in successfully defending himself against a charge of cruelty and corruption. The second is William Smith (1769–1839), who produced the first geological map of England.

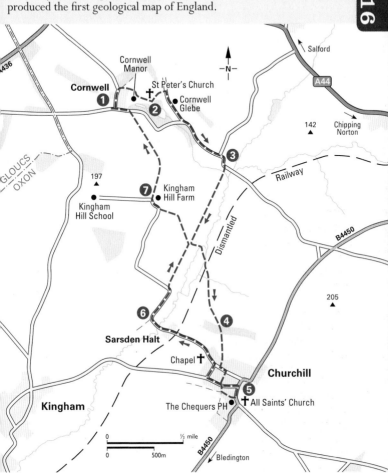

WALK 16 DIRECTIONS

❶ Turn left and walk down and up through Cornwell. Pass a farm, right, and turn right, signposted 'D'Arcy Dalton Way'. Where the track veers left, keep ahead, by a fingerpost. Walk down an orchard bearing left. Go through the hedge at the corner, and immediately through a metal gate on your left. Turn right and walk downhill. Go

though a gate, right; follow the path towards St Peter's Church.

❷ Go through a gate into the churchyard. Pass the church, and leave via a squeeze gate. Walk straight ahead down the hill, cross the bridge at the bottom and go up to the gate. Turn right along the road, passing Cornwell Glebe. Bear left along the road and pass a left turning to Salford.

3 Turn right along a bridleway, signed 'Kingham'. Follow this for 0.5 mile (800m), go through a gate on the left and walk ahead down the field-edge. Cross a footbridge, go through a gate, and follow the path diagonally right. Cross another footbridge and bear right along the stream. Soon bear left and go through a gate. Cross the track and a footbridge opposite and bear diagonally right across the field corner. Cross a footbridge in a hedge and continue on through two fields.

4 Cross a stile into the woods. Follow the path down, over a footbridge and right up the other side. Go through a gate and ahead towards Churchill. Cross a stile, then bear right beside a house. Cross a stile and turn left up the road. Pass a postbox and turn right along a path. At the next road turn left. At the top turn right.

5 Turn right again before you reach the church and follow the path round the back of The Chequers pub. Pass a barn and maintain your direction into a field. Soon turn right through a gate and walk down a grassy lane. At the road turn left; turn right at the next junction, then left at the end. Follow this road out of the village, passing the old chapel, now a heritage centre. Continue through Sarsden Halt.

6 Follow the road right, then keep straight ahead along the green lane. After 0.3 mile (480m) go through a gate on your left and bear diagonally up the field. Walk up the hedge and turn right along the road.

7 Continue walking straight ahead through Kingham Hill Farm. Pass through a gate at the other side and carry on straight across two fields. Cross a stile, then a footbridge and stile and keep straight on. Pass an old gate and continue diagonally left up the field. Pass a marker post and continue through a gate bearing slightly right over the hill crest. Take the gate to the left of the main gate and turn left up the road to return to your car and the start of the walk.

Wanderings at Wychwood

*A gentle walk through rolling Oxfordshire farmland
and a corner of an ancient forest.*

DISTANCE 5.75 miles (9.2km) **MINIMUM TIME** 3hrs

ASCENT/GRADIENT 574ft (175m) ▲▲▲ **LEVEL OF DIFFICULTY** ✦✦✦

PATHS Field paths, quiet roads, woodland tracks, no stiles

LANDSCAPE Gently rolling hills of arable farmland, ancient woods

SUGGESTED MAP OS Explorer 180 Oxford, Witney & Woodstock

START / FINISH Grid reference: SP 318194

DOG FRIENDLINESS Lead essential for road stretches, otherwise excellent

PARKING On village street near phone box, Chilson

PUBLIC TOILETS None en route

The Wychwood takes its name from a local Saxon tribe, the Hwicce. At the time of the Norman conquest, Wychwood Forest was one of four royal hunting grounds in England, and covered most of western Oxfordshire. The leafy remains of this once magnificent demesne are now mostly confined to the hilltops that lie between Ascott-under-Wychwood, Charlbury, Ramsden and Leafield, and private land ownership means that access for walkers is sometimes frustratingly limited.

A National Nature Reserve

At its heart is a National Nature Reserve, which preserves some 360 species of wild flowers and ferns, including the elusive yellow star of Bethlehem and the bizarre toothwort, a parasitic plant that is found on the roots of some trees. This walk takes you through the edge of the old woodland, on a path that in spring is carpeted with drifts of bluebells that stretch away as far as you can see. The rich variety of wild flowers means a corresponding abundance of butterflies, including peacock, tortoiseshell and orange tip.

The Shrinking Forest

By 1300 the once-flourishing 'forest' had been split into three sections: Woodstock, based around the royal hunting lodge first built here during the reign of Ethelred II; the area around Cornbury Park; and a section around Witney, where the Bishop of Winchester had built his palace. The forest continued to decline and, by 1857, only 10 square miles (26sq km) were left. As the enclosure of land became commonplace in the 1860s, Kingstanding Farm, passed on this walk, was one of seven new farms built at this time to take advantage of the newly available land.

The Ascott Martyrs

The village of Ascott-under-Wychwood is tucked in the valley below the remnants of the Wychwood, along with its near-neighbours Shipton-under-Wychwood and Milton-under-Wychwood. Ascott may not be the prettiest village, but it has another claim to fame: the Ascott Martyrs. These 16 young women played their part in the Agricultural Revolution of the 19th century when, in 1873, they attempted to dissuade Ramsden men from taking over the jobs of local men, who had been sacked for membership of the Agricultural Workers' Union. Indeed, the women were accused of encouraging the imported labourers to join the same union. Their punishment – imprisonment with hard labour – caused a riot outside the court in Chipping Norton and the women had to be secretly transferred to Oxford gaol. Their sentences were later remitted by Queen Victoria and some accounts say she sent each woman a red flannel petticoat and five shillings. The union presented them with blue silk for dresses and £5 each.

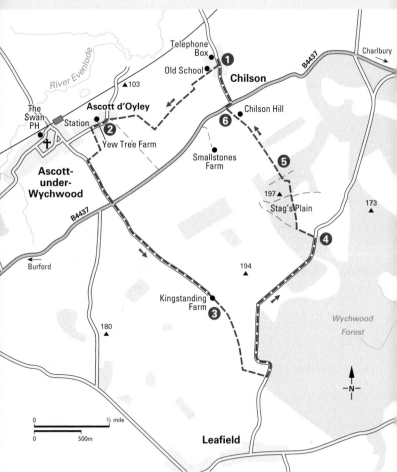

WALK 17 DIRECTIONS

1 From the phone box, turn south along the village street, and right up School Lane, passing various houses and the Old School at the end, on the right. Follow the bridleway straight on into the

field ahead, with the hedge to your right, passing through two gates. Stay on the path round the edge of the field as it kinks left then right. Keep straight on, descend steadily, and follow as the track bends right. At the hedge turn right then immediately left through a gateway; take the track diagonally left across the field (if the track has been ploughed over keep right round the edge of the field) towards Ascott-under-Wychwood, to meet a lane.

2 Turn left along the lane through Ascott d'Oyley, passing Yew Tree Farmhouse on the right. Beyond d'Oyley House and just before a recreation ground turn left up a track, Priory Lane, which becomes a grassy path under trees. It bends sharp right, and emerges at a road by a house. Turn left up the road, and cross the main road at the top with care. Continue straight ahead up the lane, signed 'Restricted byway'. Follow this straight uphill for a mile (1.6km), to pass through the buildings of Kingstanding Farm.

3 Continue down the stony track and keep straight on. It leads along the bottom of a winding, secret valley, with the solid spire of Leafield church up to your right. Emerge at a main road; turn left and follow the road as it snakes uphill, with Wychwood Forest to your right. After about 1 mile (1.6km) the road descends into woodland. As it ascends again, look for a wooden gate on the left, signed 'Circular Walk Footpath'.

4 Turn left through here and follow the track up the edge of the woods. Keep right and cross the clearing of Stag's Plain. Bend

left and right and continue on the track through the woods, carpeted with bluebells in spring.

5 Start to descend and emerge from the woods. Continue straight ahead, following the track downhill, with a hedge on your right. Pass Smallstones Farm, over to the left. Bend left at the bottom of the field, pass a wooden fence, and take the path that leads to the left, down the hill and past Chilson Hill cottage (right).

6 At the bottom of the drive turn right along the main road and immediately left down the road that leads into Chilson village. Enter the village and keep straight on past the tiny triangular green, passing the old Primitive Methodist chapel on your left. Pass the end of School Lane and return to your car.

A Final Folly
in Faringdon

*Visit an intriguing Gothic tower before venturing
into open countryside.*

DISTANCE 7.5 miles (12.1km)   MINIMUM TIME 3hrs

ASCENT/GRADIENT 115ft (35m) ▲▲▲   LEVEL OF DIFFICULTY +++

PATHS Roads (mostly quiet), field paths, drives and tracks, 15 stiles

LANDSCAPE Gently rolling farmland

SUGGESTED MAP OS Explorer 170 Abingdon, Wantage

START/FINISH Grid reference: SU 286956

DOG FRIENDLINESS On lead where indicated

PARKING Long stay car park off Gloucester Street, Faringdon

PUBLIC TOILETS Southampton Street car park (by The Bell Hotel)

Britain's follies are fascinating, their exuberance and eccentricity often reflecting the character of those who built them. A typical example is Gerald Tyrwhitt-Wilson, 14th Lord Berners (1883–1950), whose name alone conjures up images of the stereotypical upper-class twit or chinless wonder immortalised in old, much-loved British comedy films.

Widely regarded as Britain's last major folly tower and very much a local landmark, Faringdon Folly dates back to 1935. While out walking on Folly Hill one day, Lord Berners turned to his companion, Robert Heber-Percy, and commented that the hill would look even better with a folly built on it. Berners was far from conventional. He was, in every sense of the word, a gay lord – colourful, generous, talented, amusing and unmarried. Berners embodied all the characteristics of the classic British eccentric. Typically, whatever he did was characterised by a dash of mischief.

Aside from his sense of fun and dry mocking humour, Berners was one of life's naturally gifted players. He was an accomplished writer, painter and composer – Stravinsky called him the best British composer of the 20th century and Diaghilev commissioned him to compose the score for the ballet *Triumph of Neptune*. During his time at Faringdon House, he hosted many glittering parties and among his regular guests were some of the most talented figures of the pre-war arts world.

Word quickly spread that Berners was planning to build on the hill, provoking strong opposition among neighbouring landowners. Berners won his battle, however, and completion of the 100ft (30m) tower was marked by a spectacular party and fireworks display on 5 November.

Faringdon Folly is a curious mix of styles. Berners commissioned his friend Lord Wellesley to build the tower, choosing a Gothic design which the architect deplored. While Berners was abroad, Wellesley began construction work, but when his client returned he discovered the tower bore no resemblance to his specification. Instead it followed classical lines. Berners immediately ordered that the tower be completed in ornate Gothic. Robert Heber-Percy, who lived with Lord Berners at Faringdon House, gifted the tower to the town of Faringdon in 1983.

Buckland

`A420`

`B4508`

Church of
Mary The Virgin

✝ **C**

Buckland
House ✝

The
Lamb
Inn

Birch Hill

→ Hatford

B ● Dovecote

Home
Farm

116
▲

Golf
Course

St Hugh's School

Golf Course

Rushey Cottage

A

3

BARCOTE   LANE

Tagdown Barn

Barcote
Manor

Hatford
Gorse

Barcote
Park

Littleworth

4

Wadley
Lodge

←—N—
|

▲121

72
▲

Haremoor
Farm

2 `A420`

`A417`

Grove Lodge

Folly

0   ½ mile
0   500m

STANFORD RD

Church
Path Farm

The Bell Hotel

1 P

✝

`A4095`

`A417`

`B4019`

Faringdon Park

Faringdon

`A417`

WALK 18

WALK 18 DIRECTIONS

1 Follow the car park exit road and turn left at the T-junction. Make for the town centre, following Gloucester Street along to Cornmarket. Pass The Red Lion and The Bell Hotel, cross the Market Place by keeping to the right side and pass The Folly pub. Turn right into Stanford Road, then left at the sign for Folly Hill. Take the path, following it as it begins a moderate climb to Faringdon Folly. Keep to the right of the tower, emerge from the trees and continue ahead down the slope to a stile. Go straight ahead across the field to a stile leading out to the A420 road.

WHAT TO LOOK OUT FOR

As you reach the end of the walk, look out for All Saints' parish church. The Pye Chapel recalls Henry Pye who was Lord of the Manor here when George III made him Poet Laureate.

2 Cross over to a stile and go ahead, but on reaching a new plantation among older trees, bear half right, aiming to strike the Wadley Lodge drive to the left of a defunct white gate. Now with a pond well to your right, aim for a distant white metal gate. Keep left here, following trees and bushes along the field-edge. Make for the corner and pass through a gap to continue ahead on the bridleway, cutting across fields with woodland over to the right. This is Hatford Gorse and just beyond it

WHERE TO EAT AND DRINK

In Faringdon pubs include The Bell Hotel and The Red Lion; bakers or sandwich bars for snacks. On the walk extension is The Lamb Inn at Buckland.

is the dilapidated Tagdown Barn. Follow the bridleway to a house and join the road on a hairpin bend. Keep ahead to a left curve. The bridleway runs straight on, part of Walk 19.

WHILE YOU'RE THERE

Make time to explore Faringdon. King Alfred (see Walk 23) had a royal manor here and King John granted a charter for a market.

3 Follow the lane to the A420, cross over and take the drive ahead towards Barcote Park. Turn left at the footpath sign and cross the field to two stiles in the line of trees. Cross them and turn right along the field edge for 50yds (46m) to the next stile. Go down the field and through a line of trees to two stiles and head up the slope to a kissing gate. Walk beside a fenced playing field then join a drive to the road, turn right and walk through the village of Littleworth.

4 As the road bends sharp right by Hill House, go through the gate marked Chapel House, signposted 'Church Walk Faringdon'. Follow the track to the right for a few paces to a stile and gate. Take the path west across the field, with Faringdon Folly in the distance. This field is over 0.5 mile (800m) across! Cross a stile, keep to the right of the farm outbuildings, negotiate two stiles with a track in between and walk ahead. Make for gates in the field corner, continue ahead in the next pasture and approach a house. Keep to the right of it, walk for a 0.25 mile (400m) between hedge and fence, then join a farm track towards Faringdon. Continue ahead on the road and round to the Market Place. Return to the car park.

The Beauty of Buckland

Visit a picturesque village dominated by a splendid 18th-century house.

See map and information panel for Walk 18

| DISTANCE 10 miles (16.1km) | MINIMUM TIME 4hrs |
| ASCENT/GRADIENT 115ft (35m) ▲▲▲ | LEVEL OF DIFFICULTY +++ |

WALK 19 DIRECTIONS
(Walk 18 option)

As the road bends left, Point **Ⓐ**, walk ahead along the bridleway, following it across the fields towards trees and the semi-wooded slopes of a golf course. Join an enclosed path running beside a young plantation and pass through a gate into the mixed woodland. Go ahead for 700yds (640m) to a track crossroads. Turn left to skirt woodland. This curves right, passing to the side of a galvanised gate, and soon there is tarmac underfoot. Keep ahead to the complex of extensive converted outbuildings at Home Farm, Point **Ⓑ**.

On the right is an octagonal dovecote, which has also been given a new lease of life. Keep ahead on the drive to the busy A420 road. Cross over to a footpath sign, gate and lodge. Walk ahead for a few paces to a stile, then cross the parkland with a wire fence on your left. Buckland House can be seen in the distance. Cross a stile and follow the path through woodland to the road. Turn left into Buckland, passing The Lamb Inn on the left. On reaching a T-junction, Point **Ⓒ**, go straight over to visit the Church of St Mary the Virgin, which contains various manorial box pews, hatchment boards and brasses, and an alabaster carving of the Adoration of the Shepherds. Return to this point, turn right towards Witney and immediately pass the Roman Catholic church.

Beyond it is a very good view of Buckland House, built by the Throckmorton family in the mid-18th century. With its central block of mellow stone and octagonal pavilions at either end, one formerly a chapel and the other a library, the house is a perfect example of neoclassical architecture. The estate includes a large lake and a deer park of 150 acres (61ha). Buckland House is not open to the public.

Pass the main entrance to the house and keep ahead to the T-junction. Cross over and follow a bridleway across the fields. Eventually you reach a canopy of trees. Keep ahead, following the waymarked path through the grounds of St Hugh's School. Look for hard tennis courts and a ha-ha before reaching the road. Turn right, then left just beyond Rushey Cottage, joining a bridleway which cuts across the fields. At Barcote Park drive rejoin Walk 18.

The Ewelme Chaucers

A downland walk to an historic church associated with a famous poet's family.

DISTANCE *4 miles (6.4km)* **MINIMUM TIME** *1hr 30min*

ASCENT/GRADIENT *164ft (50m)* ▲▲▲ **LEVEL OF DIFFICULTY** +++

PATHS *Farm tracks, paths and roads (can be busy in Ewelme)*

LANDSCAPE *Spectacular downland*

SUGGESTED MAP *OS Explorer 171 Chiltern Hills West*

START/FINISH *Grid reference: SU 648912*

DOG FRIENDLINESS *On lead in Ewelme, under control near livestock*

PARKING *Small car park by sports ground at Ewelme*

PUBLIC TOILETS *None en route*

WALK 20 DIRECTIONS

Take the footpath which begins parallel to the road towards Swyncombe and Cookley Green. Ease away from the hedge to a kissing gate in trees. Turn left for 150yds (137m, not less) then right, between stone pillars and wrought-iron and gilt gates, towards Ewelme Down Farm.

Keep to the main track, following it for well over 0.5 mile (800m). Pass the farm outbuildings and continue between trees and hedgerows. Turn left at an intersection at the end of a right-hand curve, indicated by a low waymarker beside two chestnut trees, about 0.25 mile (400m) from the farm, and head north, along a left-hand boundary. In the next field continue with the hedge now on your right.

On reaching the road, turn right and when, after a short distance, it bends right, go straight on along the edge of a pretty beechwood. This is the route of the Icknield Way, an ancient highway. Turn left after a few paces and follow the Chiltern Way over open fields and downland. Keep ahead, through a ribbon plantation towards farm outbuildings and a house. Pass to the left of them continuing for 700yds (640m), to where the main track bends right at some double gates. Go ahead for 0.5 mile (800m) along the lesser way between fences and new hedgerow to a road.

Turn left, pass the Ewelme village sign and a bridleway on the right, and make for the village centre. Cross Hampden Way and follow the road as it sweeps sharp right, avoiding the turning to the church. Pass Chaucer Court on the right and the site of the old village pound where stray horses and cattle were held.

WHERE TO EAT AND DRINK

The Shepherds Hut is just outside Ewelme village centre. The menu includes light snacks and main meals (no food on Sunday evening). Outside there is a large beer garden.

EWELME

It was probably last in use immediately prior to the Second World War.

Turn left at the T-junction towards Swyncombe and Crowmarsh, passing a pond on the left. This is Ewelme High Street. Just before the road bends sharp right, turn left into Burrows Hill and begin a moderate but brief climb to Ewelme churchyard and the road.

WHAT TO LOOK OUT FOR

Beside the path to the Old Rectory, adjoining the church, is the grave of Jerome K Jerome, best known for his wonderful book about a Thames journey, *Three Men in a Boat* (1889).

Among the village's most historic and distinctive buildings is the early 15th-century church, St Mary's, which featured in the television filming of John Mortimer's *Paradise Postponed*. Step inside and have a look at the church's many treasures before finishing the walk.

As you enter the church, look for the altar tomb which lies in St John's Chapel between the first and second bays of the chancel. The tomb is that of Thomas Chaucer, who died in 1434, and his wife Matilda Burghersh, who died two years later. Thomas was the son of Geoffrey Chaucer, the poet, and his mother was Philippa Roet, whose sister was the third wife of John of Gaunt, son of Edward III.

The marble slab is decorated with the brasses of Thomas in plate armour, with the unicorn crest at his feet. In each corner is a shield of arms. On the sides of the tomb is one of the largest and most fascinating displays of medieval shields of arms to be found anywhere in the country. The shields and the inscription were restored in 1843 and are thought to date back to the 1430s.

Another imposing tomb in the church is that of Alice, Duchess of Suffolk. Daughter of Thomas and Matilda, Alice died in 1475. Alice inherited the manor of Ewelme from her mother and, after marrying William de la Pole, the Duke of Suffolk, she and her husband planned to transform Ewelme into a model medieval village. However, the Duke did not live to see the fruits of his labour. In 1450, while on his way to France, the Duke was brutally murdered. His widow took charge of the work at Ewelme, supervising the building of the school and almshouses and the rebuilding of the church. When Queen Victoria became Sovereign of the Order of the Garter, it was uncertain as to where a lady should wear the garter. To try and resolve the matter, it was decided to inspect the tombs of those who wore the Garter. Among them was the effigy of the Duchess of Suffolk. Alice is depicted wearing the Order of the Garter on her left wrist.

WHILE YOU'RE THERE

Allow time to look round Ewelme. The village is renowned for its watercress beds. A leisurely tour of Ewelme's quiet streets and hidden corners reveals an assortment of architectural styles.

After visiting the church, turn right and pass the Old Rectory. Continue down the lane and out of the village. Cross over at the next junction, and back to the car park.

Overleaf: Shady woods in the grounds of Blenheim Palace (Walk 21)

Blenheim Palace Parkland

A fine walk in peaceful countryside to one of Britain's top country houses.

DISTANCE *7 miles (11.3km)*   **MINIMUM TIME** *3hrs*

ASCENT/GRADIENT *150ft (46m)* ▲▲▲   **LEVEL OF DIFFICULTY** ✚✚✚

PATHS *Field paths and tracks, parkland paths and estate drives. Some quiet road walking, 2 stiles*

LANDSCAPE *Farmland and parkland*

SUGGESTED MAP *OS Explorer 180 Oxford*

START/FINISH *Grid reference: SP 412159*

DOG FRIENDLINESS *On lead in grounds of Blenheim Palace*

PARKING *Spaces in centre of Combe*

PUBLIC TOILETS *Blenheim Palace, for visitors; otherwise none en route*

When King George III first set eyes on Blenheim Palace, he remarked, 'We have nothing to equal this.' Few would disagree with him. The views of the palace, the lake and the Grand Bridge from the waterside path on this delightful walk are stunning. Set in a magnificent 2,000-acre (810ha) park landscaped by 'Capability' Brown, the great Baroque house covers a staggering 7 acres (2.8ha) and is England's largest stately home.

Blenheim Palace took nearly 20 years to build and was finally completed in 1722. The architect John Vanbrugh was commissioned to design the house for John Churchill, 1st Duke of Marlborough (1650–1722), following his victory over the French at Blenheim in 1704. Inside, there are various state rooms and tapestries, the Long Library – considered by many to be the finest room in the house – and the room where Winston Churchill was born in 1874 (see Walk 22).

A Just Reward

It was Queen Anne who decided that John Churchill's efforts in battle should be suitably rewarded, reflecting the high regard in which the nation held him. But what exactly did Churchill do to earn such respect? As a soldier and as a statesman, he was responsible for supressing Louis XIV's imperialist ambitions in Europe. His spirit and determination resulted in a humiliating defeat of the French at Blenheim on 13 August 1704.

In gratitude, Queen Anne conferred the Royal Manor of Woodstock on the Duke of Marlborough and his heirs in perpetuity, and a sum of £500,000 was voted by parliament for the building of Blenheim Palace. But problems lay ahead. The Duke's wife, Sarah, was Princess Anne's favourite companion before she became Queen in 1702. Sarah used her close friendship and her influence in royal circles to secure a dukedom for her husband, and it was she, not the Duke of Marlborough, who approved the plans and then supervised the building work. Proving just how ruthless and determined she could be, Sarah rejected Sir Christopher Wren's designs in favour of those produced by John Vanbrugh.

BLENHEIM PALACE

A Sweet House

The Duchess remained a thorn in the side of builders and architects for some time, insisting that all she wanted was a 'clean, sweet house and garden, be it ever so small.' Parliament complained about the spiralling cost, money gradually ran out and the Duchess forbade Vanbrugh from seeing the finished building in 1725, refusing him entry to the grounds.

Characterised by ornament and exuberance, creating a memorable skyline, Blenheim Palace is not to everyone's taste, though the immense scale of the house has to be seen as a tribute to the skill and ingenuity of its creators. The vast parkland and gardens, too, are renowned for their beauty and range with Vanbrugh's Grand Bridge as the focal point.

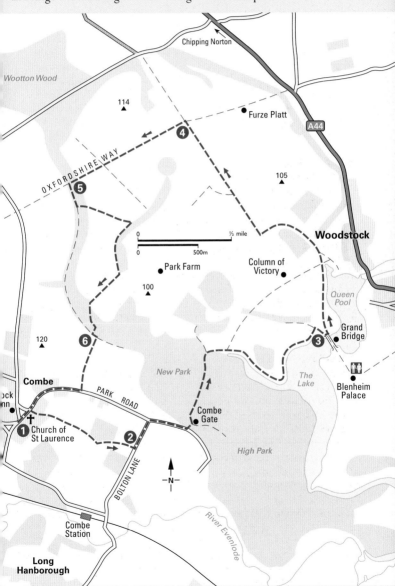

WALK 21 DIRECTIONS

1 From the green, take the road signposted 'East End'. Swing right by the village pump into the churchyard and keep left of the church. Exit through the gap in the boundary wall, flanked by two gravestones, and begin skirting the right-hand edge of the sports field. After about 50yds (46m), branch off into the trees, then head diagonally across the field. Cross into the next field and keep to the right edge of the wood. In the next field, turn left (trees on the left) and go up to the woodland corner. Pass through a gap in the hedge and cross the field.

2 Exit to the road, turn left and keep right at the next junction. Walk to Combe Gate. Go through the large kissing gate into the grounds of Blenheim Palace, keep left at the junction and follow the drive through the parkland. As it sweeps left to a cattle grid, veer to the right by a Public Footpath sign. Follow the grassy path to a stile. Keep right when the path divides and walk beside the western arm of The Lake.

3 Eventually you reach a tarmac drive. Turn right and walk down towards the Grand Bridge. As you approach it, turn sharp left, passing between mature trees with Queen Pool on your right. Cross a cattle grid and keep ahead through the park. With the Column of Victory on your left, follow the drive as it sweeps to the right.

4 Turn left at the second cattle grid, in line with Furze Platt (right). Join the Oxfordshire Way, go through a gate and follow the grassy track beside trees, then along a gravel track between fields. At length cross a track and continue towards woodland. Enter, and turn left after a few paces to join a clear track.

5 After about 150yds (137m) take the first left, crossing a footbridge to reach a field edge. Keep right here, following the obvious path across a large field beside fencing. When you reach a track, turn right. Keep alongside trees to a junction. Turn right and follow the grassy track down to and through a wood, then diagonally left across a strip of pasture to an opening. Go up to a track and cross it to a ladder stile.

6 Turn left to a hedge, then turn right, keeping it and a ditch on your right. Skirt a field to the road, turn right and walk back into Combe.

WHILE YOU'RE THERE

Have a look at Combe church. The original building, which was in the valley about 1 mile (1.6km) from its present site, was built during the Norman period. The present church was built in about 1395, about 50 years after the villagers moved their homes out of the valley. The design of the church is an example of the Early Perpendicular style, with a stone pulpit and medieval stained glass.

Churchill's Grave at Bladon

Take a walk to the heart of rural Oxfordshire, visiting the final resting place of Britain's most famous statesman.

DISTANCE 5 miles (8km)   **MINIMUM TIME** 2hrs 15min

ASCENT/GRADIENT 90ft (27m) ▲▲▲   **LEVEL OF DIFFICULTY** ✦✦✦

PATHS Field and woodland paths and tracks, quiet roads, 8 stiles

LANDSCAPE Farmland and woodland on east bank of River Evenlode

SUGGESTED MAP OS Explorer 180 Oxford

START/FINISH Grid reference: SP 468138

DOG FRIENDLINESS Under control on farmland and on lead where requested

PARKING Limited spaces outside Begbroke church, St Michael's Lane

PUBLIC TOILETS None en route

One name remains synonymous with Britain's victory over the Nazi regime in 1945 – that of Sir Winston Churchill. And yet if it had not been for the Second World War, Churchill would have been almost forgotten by now, his political record meaning little, if anything, in today's world. His shifting allegiance between the Conservative and Liberal parties might have given him a slightly higher profile, but that is all.

Instead, he came into his own as Britain's wartime leader, renowned for his inspired rhetoric and his familiar 'V for victory' salute. He so perfectly embodied the fighting spirit and determination of the British character and, as well as being a magnificent statesman, he was probably the greatest orator of modern times.

A Great Man is Born

Churchill was born at Blenheim Palace (see Walk 21) in 1874. He was educated at Harrow and Sandhurst and took part in the charge of the 21st Lancers at the Battle of Omdurman before becoming a newspaper correspondent in the Boer War. In 1900 he entered parliament as a Tory MP but later crossed the floor of the House to join the Liberal majority.

As Home Secretary he witnessed the famous Siege of Sidney Street and, as First Lord of the Admiralty, with the threat of the First World War looming, he began strengthening Britain's military arsenal, becoming Minister of Munitions in 1917. However, between the wars he found himself in the political wilderness, with his concern over the increasing Nazi threat largely ignored.

The dark days of 1940 eventually dawned and Neville Chamberlain stepped down as Prime Minister, heralding Churchill's 'walk with destiny'. Not only would this be Britain's finest hour, but Churchill's too – the zenith of his political career. He began shaping the 1941 Atlantic Charter, looked to America for help and support in the war and masterminded the strategy adopted for the Battle of Britain, Alamein and the North African campaign. With the war won, a victorious Churchill went to the country, hoping for a landslide result. But it was not to be. He lost the election to Labour.

WALK 22

Churchill's Last Years

In 1951, six years after losing the election, Churchill was returned to power. He won the Nobel Prize for Literature in 1953, but had quite a severe stroke in the same year. With Britain's post-war recovery well advanced, he eventually retired as Prime Minister in 1955, his health by now in dramatic decline. He died ten years later, and at the express wish of the Queen was the first commoner since Wellington to be afforded a state funeral. Churchill's death not only represented the passing of a momentous era but came to be acknowledged as the end of the British Empire.

Seventy years earlier, aged 20, Churchill wrote to his mother: 'I went this morning to Bladon to look at Papa's grave...I was so struck by the sense of quietness and peace, as well as by the old-world air of the place, that my sadness was not unmixed with solace...'

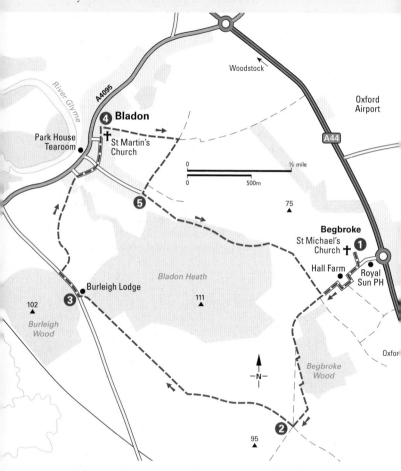

WALK 22 DIRECTIONS

❶ Keep the church behind you, walk along to Spring Hill Road and turn right. Follow the lane through two sharp bends, passing

Hall Farm. Avoid the path on the right and continue ahead to a stile and some galvanised gates. Follow the track up a gentle slope and on to the next stile and a cattle grid. Keep ahead, passing a stone-built house on the left, and then swing right across the field, passing under telegraph wires. Pass into the next field and turn right.

2 Follow the obvious boundary across three fields, eventually turning left in the corner. Continue for about 50yds (46m) and look for a stile and footbridge on the right. Keep ahead in the next field, with the hedge on the left. On reaching the field corner, go forward for a few paces, then turn right through an opening in the hedge into the adjoining field. Maintain the same direction as before, with the boundary on your left. Make for a stile and oak tree in the field corner. Continue ahead across the next field, keeping to the left edge of woodland. With trees hard by you on the right, follow the path towards Burleigh Lodge. Swing left for a few paces to a stile leading out to the road.

WHILE YOU'RE THERE

Have a look at Bladon's parish Church of St Martin. There has been a church on this site for over 800 years. The place oozes history – Henry II and Thomas Becket walked together here, Edward the Black Prince grew up here and Elizabeth I was imprisoned near by.

---

3 Turn right by the millennium stone, pass the lodge and walk along the road to a footpath sign on the right for Bladon. Cross the stile and keep the hedge on the left. Make for a stile and footbridge in the field corner, turn left and follow the hedgerow. Look for a hedge running diagonally right, keep it on your left and head towards the rooftops of Bladon. Make for a stile leading out to the road on a bend. Go forward, bear right at

new housing, continue to the next junction and cross over to Church Street. Walk along to the Church of St Martin and head through the churchyard, passing Winston Churchill's grave, to the gate on the far side.

WHERE TO EAT AND DRINK

The Royal Sun at Begbroke, a few minutes on foot from the start and finish of the walk, offers traditional Sunday lunches, main meals and snacks. Park House Tea Rooms beside the A4095 in Bladon serves tea, cakes, sandwiches and hot meals.

---

4 Turn right and follow the tarmac lane to wooden gates. Continue ahead on the field path to the corner and turn right at the waymark. With a hedgerow on the left, pass to the left of woodland and head for a white gate. At the road beyond, turn left past lock-up garages and follow the path signposted to Begbroke.

5 Cross a rectangular pasture and, at the far end, follow the path into the trees and through a gate. Emerge at length from the wood at another gate and continue ahead along the field boundary towards Begbroke. Go through a gate in the corner and follow the path alongside the drive to the road. Turn left and left again into St Michael's Lane, returning to the church.

WHAT TO LOOK OUT FOR

Visitors from all corners of the world visit Churchill's final resting place at Bladon, expressing their gratitude and admiration for the leadership qualities of this legendary statesman in the visitor book and on his grave.

Alfred's Greatness Remembered at Wantage

Visit the statue of a revered British king before heading for spectacular downland country.

DISTANCE 5.25 miles (8.4km)   MINIMUM TIME 2hrs 30min

ASCENT/GRADIENT 150ft (46m) ▲▲▲   LEVEL OF DIFFICULTY +++

PATHS Pavements, tow path, field paths and tracks, 1 stile

LANDSCAPE Town outskirts, farmland and downland

SUGGESTED MAP OS Explorer 170 Abingdon, Wantage

START/FINISH Grid reference: SU 397877

DOG FRIENDLINESS On lead on town outskirts, in villages and if horses about

PARKING Portway car park (enter from Church Street)

PUBLIC TOILETS At start

King Alfred (AD 849–99) is one of those heroic figures we may remember from the pages of school history books. His victories in battle and his reputation for scholarship and justice rightly earned him the title Alfred the Great. He is suitably commemorated in the Market Place of Wantage, the town of his birth. The striking marble statue of him at its centre was sculpted by Count Gleichen, Prince of Hohenlohne-Langenburg, and unveiled in 1877. As you pass by it, in the initial stages of the walk, note the battleaxe in one hand and manuscript in the other.

Alfred Makes his Mark

Alfred, the youngest son of King Aethelwulf, succeeded his brother Aethelred as King in 871, at a time when Viking invaders had overwhelmed most of England to the north of the Thames and Wessex was under constant attack. Seven years later Alfred defeated the Danish army at Edington in Wiltshire. He repelled another invasion in 885 and captured London the following year. Alfred is also remembered for building a fleet, which earned him a reputation as 'father of the English navy,' and creating a ring of fortified strongholds around his kingdom. He was an educated man and as a child he travelled to Rome and to the Frankish court of Charles I, the Bald. He played a key role in reviving and translating many documents and was instrumental in codifying the laws of his kingdom. For example, he made a treaty which recognised the partition of England, with the Danelaw under Viking rule.

A Mighty Battle

But it is the Battle of Ashdown, not far from Wantage, fought in AD 871, with which most local people probably associate Alfred. While the Danes held Reading, it was Alfred's intention to try and entice them away from the river, which they commanded, and confront them on the downs.

Alfred and his brother Aethelred successfully encouraged the enemy to pursue them up the Kennet Valley. The two men then fell back towards the downs with the Danes in hot pursuit. Then, at Ashdown, they stood their ground. What happened next is not clear. The area surrounding the Ridgeway here was guarded by forts and perhaps Alfred looked to them for help in his quest for victory.

Alfred Wins the Day

Alfred won the day, sending the Danes packing, proving that once they were away from their boats they were an easy target. After a number of victories over the Danes Alfred was forced to retreat to the relative safety of the Somerset marshes. However, he had taken a positive first step in his efforts to resist the Vikings during the following years.

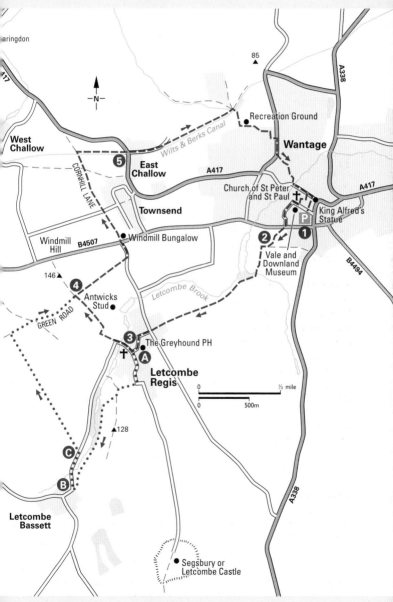

W
A
L
K

23

WALK 23 DIRECTIONS

1 Pass the public toilets, then cross Church Street to take a covered walkway to the Market Place. To the right is the statue of King Alfred, but your route is left, following the signs for the museum. Approach the parish Church of St Peter and St Paul and follow the road round to the left. Opposite you at the next junction is the Vale and Downland Museum (this is Church Street again). Turn right here, following Priory Road to its end. Cross this busy road (Portway) to a footpath to the left of The Croft.

2 Follow the clear tarmac path as it runs between fences and playing fields. At length you reach a housing estate; continue ahead into Letcombe Regis and make for the junction with Courthill Road. Keep it on your left and go straight ahead, past The Greyhound pub and a thatched cottage dated 1698, to a junction (Point **A** on Walk 24).

3 Turn right by the church, signposted 'Letcombe Bassett and Lambourn' and, when the road bends sharp left, go straight ahead. After a few paces the drive bends right. Keep ahead along a path between banks of vegetation, following it as it curves right, then swings left. Pass Antwicks Stud over to the right and climb gently between trees and bushes.

4 Turn right at the next intersection and follow the tree-lined track to the road. Turn left and make for the junction. Cross over, pass alongside Windmill Bungalow and follow Cornhill Lane. Begin a gentle descent, cross a lane by a school and continue down the slope. Keep ahead to a footbridge crossing the old Wilts & Berks Canal. Turn right and follow the tow path.

5 Take great care in crossing the A417 road then follow a works access road for 200yds (183m). Move right to walk alongside a section of restored canal. On reaching a tarmac drive, turn right to a row of houses. Turn left, pass a play area and follow a rough track as it curves right. Turn left, to some lock-up garages. Go right, but soon left to a mini-roundabout. Turn right, seeking Belmont (a street) on the left. Turn here but immediately fork right into a fenced path guarded by one bollard. Follow this, passing extensive new housing, to Mill Street. Turn left, up to King Alfred's monument and the start.

Letcombe Bassett

Visit a pretty village disguised in print by one of Britain's greatest writers.

See map and information panel for Walk 23

DISTANCE *8.5 miles (13.7km)*   **MINIMUM TIME** *3hrs 30min*
ASCENT/GRADIENT *150ft (46m)* ▲▲▲   **LEVEL OF DIFFICULTY** ✦✦✦

WALK 24 DIRECTIONS
(Walk 23 option)

Turn left at the junction, Point **Ⓐ**, by Letcombe Regis church (signposted 'Village downs only'). When the road bends left, swing right at a bridleway sign and make for a gate and footpath waymark. Avoid them and keep left, after a few paces arriving at a junction of rights of way. Keep right here, following the sign for the nature trail. Ignore the stile on the left and follow the path between fence and hedge. Pass a gate leading to the nature trail and follow the delightful tree-shaded path above the Letcombe Brook. Cross a stile and eventually the path drops down to the road, Point **Ⓑ**. To visit the village of Letcombe Bassett, turn left, otherwise turn right, down the hill, over a bridge and up again.

For many years Letcombe Bassett has been closely associated with racehorse training, with strings of horses often seen making their way to the nearby gallops or in the surrounding lanes. The growing of watercress in Letcombe Brook is also a local tradition, and Letcombe Bassett has a strong literary connection.

Thomas Hardy based the village of Cresscombe on this settlement in his classic novel *Jude the Obscure*, first published in 1895. Arabella's Cottage is where Jude, hiking over the downs, stumbles on his future wife washing pig's chitterlings in the local stream. She attracts Jude's attention by lobbing part of the pig at him, signalling the beginning of Jude's downfall. Hardy selected nearby towns and villages to appear in the story: Fawley and Wantage became Marygreen and Alfredston respectively, and Oxford (see Walk 8) was thinly disguised as Christminster.

Letcombe Bassett is also associated with another writer. Jonathan Swift, who wrote *Gulliver's Travels*, visited the village in 1714 at the invitation of the rector. It is said he occupied his time writing under a mulberry tree in the Old Rectory garden.

Pass a thatched cottage, Point **Ⓒ**, and turn left just beyond it, signposted 'bridleway'. Follow the bridleway between the fields and after a little over 0.75 mile (1.2km) you come to a junction with a track known as Green Road. Turn right and follow this for a little under 0.5 mile (800m) to rejoin Walk 23 at the next junction.

Ardington
– Country Estate

*This delightful walk makes for a village that was once
a centre for cloth.*

DISTANCE 5.5 miles (8.8km)   MINIMUM TIME 1hr 45min

ASCENT/GRADIENT 164ft (50m) ▲▲▲   LEVEL OF DIFFICULTY ✦✦✦

PATHS Bridleways, field paths and quiet roads, 3 stiles

LANDSCAPE Open landscape at foot of downs and Ridgeway

SUGGESTED MAP OS Explorer 170 Abingdon, Wantage

START Grid reference: SU 431884

DOG FRIENDLINESS On lead in villages, under control between

PARKING Free car parks at, and opposite, Loyd-Lindsay Rooms in Ardington;
groups of walkers should phone ahead (01235) 820054

PUBLIC TOILETS None en route

WALK 25 DIRECTIONS

The village of Ardington, with
neighbouring Lockinge, forms
part of a large self-contained
country estate established in
the 19th century by landowner
Robert Loyd-Lindsay. He fought
in the Crimea, was one of the
recipients of the Victoria Cross
and later became Baron Wantage.
Loyd-Lindsay resigned from the
army to farm the Lockinge Estate.

During the next few years,
Loyd-Lindsay rebuilt Ardington
and Lockinge as model villages,
formed a co-operative selling
good-quality food, and became
one of this area's great agricultural
pioneers, creating an enterprising
business. A *Daily News* reporter
wrote of the estate: 'It is a little
self-contained world in which
nobody is idle, nobody is in
absolute want, in which there is
no hunger or squalor.'

In 1944 the 18,000-acre
(7,290ha) estate passed to
Christopher Loyd, son of Lady

Wantage's cousin. To help clear
death and estate duties amounting
to £500,000, Loyd ordered the
Wantages' old home, in whose
gardens 50 men once worked,
to be demolished. He also sold
8,000 acres (3,240ha), a number
of cottages and many art treasures,
and moved to a smaller house
near by.

However, not all has been lost.
The social, economic and political
climate may have changed since
Baron Wantage's day, but there
have been determined efforts in
recent years to try and ensure
that the estate continues to
survive. Many of the old farm

WHILE YOU'RE THERE

Take a walk through East Hendred.
In the 16th and 17th centuries, the
village was closely associated with
cloth-making and a fair took place
annually along the Golden Mile,
stretching as far as the Ridgeway.
Many of the timber-built houses
and thatched cottages in East
Hendred date from that period.

ARDINGTON

outbuildings have been converted into craft shops, workshops, offices, a picture gallery and a pottery, helping to boost the local economy, raise the village's profile and provide much-needed employment for local people.

Next door to Ardington, Lockinge has been a venue for point-to-point meetings for 50 years. Nationally, Lockinge is one of the few courses where the original turf remains, giving perfect, fast-draining going.

From the Loyd-Lindsay Rooms walk east, passing the post office. Turn right just beyond it into Church Street. When the road curves right, turn left at the 'no horses and ponies' sign. Pass through a brick arch and follow the path to the road opposite a timber-framed cottage. Turn right, pass a turning on the left and keep left at the next track intersection.

Note the 'farm vehicles only' sign. Pass the buildings of Red Barn and, when the farm track bends right, go straight on along a grassy path between fields and through trees to reach a stile, crossing Ginge Brook. Pass West Hendred church and cross the road to a stile and a sign for East Hendred. Cross the field, keeping the fence and trees on the right-hand side, to the next stile and cross a track, following the bridleway between fences towards East Hendred.

On reaching the outskirts of the village, pass between houses and bungalows and follow Horn Lane ahead to the junction. To visit the village centre and the church, turn left. To continue the walk, turn right. Pass St Mary's Road on the left. Monks Farm House lies on the right. Keeping on the road, go up the slope between trees, to pass a grain store on your left. Then, with a turning to Aldfield Farm on the left, take the track signposted across the road, immediately beyond a belt of woodland. Follow the byway in a straight line alongside the trees and, once clear of them, keep ahead between fields.

Cross a road and continue on the next section of byway, following the edge of the field down to Ginge Brook. Cross the brook to a track and keep ahead between fields. On reaching the road on a bend, go forward and then round to the right, towards Ardington House. Cross the Ardington Brook, pass the church and turn immediately right. The entrance to Holy Trinity Church is on your right-hand side, just before you get to The Boar's Head. Pass the entrance to Ardington House on the right and make for the junction. Turn left and return to the car park.

Witney – from Town to Country

Discover Witney's many treasures before heading for a popular country park on the town's outskirts.

DISTANCE 3.5 miles (5.7km)	**MINIMUM TIME** 1hr 30min
ASCENT/GRADIENT Negligible ▲▲▲	**LEVEL OF DIFFICULTY** ✚✚✚

PATHS Pavements, meadow and waterside paths

LANDSCAPE Urban, country park and waterside on town outskirts

SUGGESTED MAP OS Explorer 180 Oxford

START/FINISH Grid reference: SP 357096

DOG FRIENDLINESS Busy streets at start and finish. Under control or on lead in Witney Lake and Meadows Country Park

PARKING Public car park by Woolgate Shopping Centre, off Witan Way

PUBLIC TOILETS Woolgate Shopping Centre, recreation ground and Cogges Manor Farm Museum (for visitors)

Unlike Burford and Broadway, Witney never established itself as a Cotswold honeypot. Perhaps it is just as well. It is a place to stumble on, to be discovered without the fuss of coach parties and souvenir hunters. Stroll through its picturesque streets and you'll find a great deal of charm and character. It is attractive without being twee, smart without being 'touristy'. In short, it is classic Middle England. One of Witney's best views is from Church Green, looking across to the parish church at the southern end. This quiet corner of the town has the feel of a small English cathedral city and if Witney were ever descended upon by tourism marketing men, the focus of their attention would surely be here.

Witney's Famous Blankets

Perhaps the main reason the town never became a major attraction is its industrial past. During the Middle Ages Witney became the centre of a thriving woollen trade. It was the famous Cotswold sheep and the meandering River Windrush that contributed to the town's success – the river proved to be eminently suitable for the scouring of the woollen cloth. Fortunately, the townsfolk knew how to yield the best from these attributes and in later years Witney became famous throughout the world for producing blankets.

It was in 1669 that Richard Early apprenticed his teenage son, Thomas, to the woollen trade. The boy lived up to his father's expectations and by 1688 he was one of the town's leading master weavers. Indeed, he was so successful that he was chosen to present a pair of gold-fringed blankets to James II. In 1711 the Witney weavers were granted a charter to form a Company of Blanket Weavers. This significant development, though long overdue, was welcomed by the district's weaving community, and weavers operating within a 20-mile (32km) radius of the town were required to bring their blankets to the company's headquarters to be inspected and hallmarked.

WITNEY

Thomas Early became the first master of the company and in later years the Early family presented blankets to King George III and Queen Charlotte as part of their royal visit to Oxfordshire in 1788. However, it wasn't long before the Industrial Revolution got under way and the wind of change began to blow through Witney, as innovative machinery ushered in a new era in the manufacturing industries. The traditional weavers feared for their jobs and riots broke out in the streets. But it was to no avail – in spite of all the protests, the new order was here to stay.

In 1960 Witney's two major blanket manufacturers merged, consolidating an association already forged by marriage between the families. With the eventual closure of the company, Witney's tradition for producing blankets now lies at the core of the town's industrial heritage.

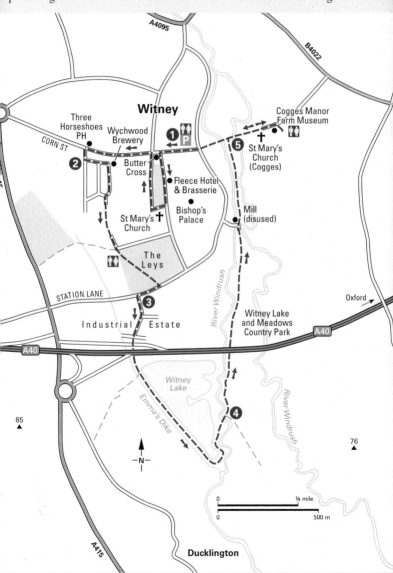

WALK 26

WALK 26 DIRECTIONS

1 Turn right into Langdale Gate and walk towards the Butter Cross. Turn left before it and walk down Church Green, passing The Fleece. Have a look at the Bishop's Palace and visit St Mary's Church next door. With your back to the church, continue along the left side of Church Green and turn left at the Butter Cross into Corn Street. Keep ahead and turn left just beyond the Three Horseshoes pub into The Crofts. Follow the road between stone houses.

WHERE TO EAT AND DRINK

The Fleece is one of many pubs in Witney. Expect a buzzy atmosphere and good food, including breakfast from 8.30. There are several cafés and restaurants in the town.

---

2 Follow The Crofts to the left and turn right at the end to pass the Wychwood Brewery. Keep a stone wall on the left and walk to St Mary's Court. Continue ahead along an alleyway, with the spire of St Mary's on the left and, when you reach the corner of a recreation ground, keep to its right edge, passing a toilet block. Turn right at the road, then turn first left at the pedestrian lights into Station Lane.

3 Follow the road through an industrial estate and take the

WHAT TO LOOK OUT FOR

Witney Lake and Meadows Country Park covers 75 acres (30ha) and includes a former gravel pit, two streams of the River Windrush, fields of hay and meadowland. The park is home to wildlife such as tawny owls, sparrowhawks, and damselflies.

---

path at the end, beneath the A40. Walk ahead through a gate. The walk now cuts between Witney Lake and surrounding meadows. Continue along the lakeside path. Keep Emma's Dike right and curve to the left. On the right is the River Windrush. Make for a large concrete bridge and cross it, branching left to a kissing gate.

4 Keep the field boundary over to your left, look for a gate and follow the path to a kissing gate by the A40. Pass under it to another kissing gate and head north to a kissing gate, keeping your back to the main road. Cross over to a gate and keep ahead with office buildings seen on the left. Pass under power lines to two kissing gates. Keep ahead, passing to the right of a dilapidated mill and go through a gate. Follow

---

WHILE YOU'RE THERE

Visit the Cogges Manor Farm Museum, which illustrates how this 20-acre (8.1ha) site would have looked in the Victorian era, with traditional breeds of animals, original farm buildings and displays of farm implements and machinery. There are daily demonstrations of farm work.

---

the path between margins of vegetation and eventually you reach a spur path to Cogges Manor Farm Museum.

5 To visit the museum, turn right and follow the path and adjoining cycleway to the Priory and St Mary's Church. Continue to the adjoining museum and then retrace your steps, heading now for Witney town centre. Pass an electricity sub station on the right and walk along to the road. Cross over into Langdale Gate and return to the car park.

Burford – a Classic Cotswold Town

Discover the delights of an ancient settlement with a long history on this attractive walk through the Windrush Valley.

DISTANCE *5 miles (8km)* MINIMUM TIME *2hrs 30min*

ASCENT/GRADIENT *250ft (76m)* ▲▲▲ LEVEL OF DIFFICULTY +++

PATHS *Field and riverside paths, tracks, country roads, 7 stiles*

LANDSCAPE *Undulating Windrush Valley to the east of Burford*

SUGGESTED MAP *OS Explorer OL45 The Cotswolds*

START / FINISH *Grid reference: SP 255123*

DOG FRIENDLINESS *Under control across farmland; on lead where requested*

PARKING *Large car park to east of Windrush, near parish church*

PUBLIC TOILETS *Burford High Street*

Often described as the gateway to the Cotswolds, the picturesque town of Burford has changed little over the years. The High Street runs down between lime trees and mellow stone houses to a narrow three-arched bridge over the River Windrush. Charles II and his mistress Nell Gwynn, whose child was named the Earl of Burford, attended Burford races and stayed at the George Hotel. When she retired to Windsor, Gwynn called her home there Burford House.

An Important Trading Centre

Situated at several major east–west and north–south crossing routes, Burford has always been regarded as an important trading centre. People would pay their tolls at the twin-gabled 15th-century Tolsey, now a museum, for the right to trade in the town and it was here that the prosperous Guild of Merchants conducted their meetings. Such was their power and influence that by the Middle Ages the merchants were running Burford as if it boasted a Mayor and Corporation.

Take a leisurely stroll through the streets of the town and you'll stumble across a host of treasures – especially in the little side roads leading off the High Street. For example, the Great House in Witney Street was the largest residence in Burford when it was built about 1690. With its Georgian façade, it certainly dwarfs the other buildings in the street. The Dolls' House, dating back to 1939 and on view in the Tolsey Museum, is modelled on the Great House.

A Gem of a Church

Burford's parish church, with its slender spire, is one of the largest in Oxfordshire. Begun about 1170, it was enlarged over subsequent centuries and one of its last additions was the south porch, noted for its elaborate stonework. The west doorway is pure Norman, as is the central part of the tower, to which another stage was added in the 15th century to provide a base for the spire. Inside, the ceiling is fan vaulted and there are five medieval screens dividing various chapels.

BURFORD

Levellers Revolt

This sizeable wool church is also associated with the Civil War Levellers – 800 Parliamentarian troopers who mutinied at Salisbury over pay and then marched north to join forces with other groups. On 14 May 1649 they reached Burford where they believed they would negotiate a settlement with Fairfax, the Commander-in-Chief. However, Fairfax had different plans and at midnight he and Cromwell entered the town with 2,000 horsemen. Following a skirmish, they captured 340 men. The prisoners were held in the church where one of them carved his name on the font. Two days later, on 17 May, three ringleaders were shot in the churchyard and a fourth was forced to preach a sermon.

Speaker's House

The Priory in Priory Lane is another of Burford's historic buildings. This Elizabethan house, rebuilt in the early 1800s, still has its Tudor gables and the heraldic arms over the doorway recall William Lenthall (1591–1662) who lived here and was elected Speaker to the Long Parliament in 1640.

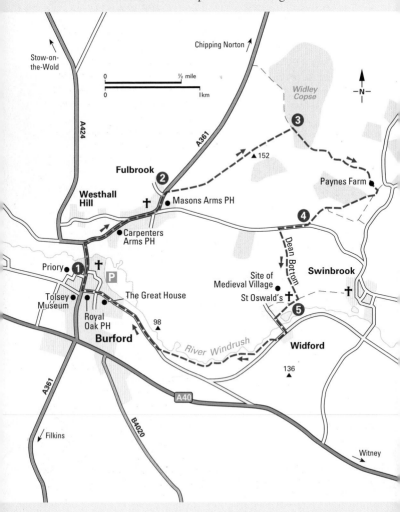

WALK 27 DIRECTIONS

1 Head north along the High Street to the Windrush. Cross the river and turn right at the mini-roundabout towards Fulbrook. Pass the Carpenters Arms and continue along the road. Avoid a turning for Swinbrook and pass the Masons Arms. Keep ahead, passing Upper End on the left, and look for a footpath on the right.

2 Follow the steps cut into the side of the slope up to the field-edge and then swing right. Follow the boundary to a waymark just before a slope and curve left to cross the field. Go through a gap in the hedge on the far side and cross the field to an opening in the hedgerow. Cross the next field towards a curtain of woodland and make for a track.

3 Keep right and follow the track through the woodland. Break cover from the trees and pass a row of cottages. Continue down the track to Paynes Farm and, just beyond it, turn right to join a signposted right of way. Head for a gate and follow the unfenced track towards trees. Descend the slope to a gate and continue ahead between hedges up the hill to the road.

4 Turn right and follow the road down into a dip. Swing left at the stile and sign for Widford and follow the grassy ride through verdant Dean Bottom. Make for a stile, turn right when you reach the T-junction and visit Widford's St Oswald's Church.

5 On leaving the church, veer right and follow the grassy track, passing a lake on the left. Turn left at the road, recross the Windrush and turn right at the junction. Keep to the road until you reach a footpath sign and stile on the right. Follow the riverside path across a series of stiles, to eventually reach the road. Turn right towards Burford, pass the Great House and the Royal Oak and return to the High Street.

Overleaf: Ivy-clad houses lining Burford's High Street

Abingdon's Architecture

Explore a former county town and then view it from a classic riverside path.

DISTANCE *7 miles (11.3km)* **MINIMUM TIME** *2hrs 45min*

ASCENT/GRADIENT *Negligible* ▲▲▲ **LEVEL OF DIFFICULTY** ✦✦✦

PATHS *Field paths and tracks, stretches of road and Thames Path. Town and village streets (roads can be busy), 4 stiles*

LANDSCAPE *Flat farmland and meadows south of Abingdon*

SUGGESTED MAP *OS Explorer 170 Abingdon, Wantage*

START/FINISH *Grid reference: SU 503941*

DOG FRIENDLINESS *On lead in Sutton Courtenay; not ideal in Abingdon*

PARKING *Small car park south of the church at Sutton Courtenay*

PUBLIC TOILETS *None at start but various in Abingdon, including Old Gaol Leisure Centre and Abbey Meadow Park*

From a distance, driving along the nearby A34, Abingdon doesn't look much. It's all business parks and out-of-town shopping centres. But leave the car behind, stroll its ancient streets and you'll be pleasantly surprised at what you find. Until 1867 Abingdon was the county town of Berkshire, later it was swallowed up when Oxfordshire greedily expanded her borders as part of the controversial county boundary changes of 1974. The town was originally developed around its famous abbey, founded in 700 and dissolved in the reign of Henry VIII. The abbey was destroyed by the Danes in the 10th century, though work began to rebuild it and William the Conqueror spent Easter here in 1084. His son Henry I appointed the Italian Abbot Foritius in 1100 and the abbey was soon acknowledged as a symbol of power and prosperity. Some of the abbey's outbuildings still remain today, including the Gateway.

Often compared to Oxford's magnificent Sheldonian Theatre (see Walk 8), the splendid Old County Hall in the Market Place was completed in 1682 by Christopher Kempster of Burford, one of Wren's master masons during the building of St Paul's Cathedral. The Old County Hall is a perfect example of English Renaissance architecture – imposing and grand for such a small town. South of the Market Place is the Old Gaol built by Napoleonic prisoners of war between 1805 and 1811.

A Soaring Landmark

The spire of the 15th-century St Helen's Church soars above the town and can be seen for miles around. The church, which is partly 13th-century, is 108ft (33m) wide and yet only 97ft (30m) long. Inside there are five aisles, a 200-year-old candelabra and a splendid medieval painted ceiling in the Lady Chapel, representing the Tree of Jesse. Next door to the church are the Long Alley Almshouses. These comprise Long Alley, Brick Alley and Twitty's. The oldest, Long Alley, dates from the mid-15th century. Diarist Samuel Pepys came here in 1668 and put a donation in the alms box.

ABINGDON

Abingdon is very much a river town, with its buildings laid out along one bank of the Thames. From the meadows on the opposite bank it is reminiscent of a seaport, with all manner of sailing craft adding a dash of colour during the summer months. Much of Abingdon's prosperity came from cloth manufacture and the historian John Leland noted in 1549 that the town 'standeth by clothing'. More recently the MG car plant provided Abingdon with employment until its eventual closure in the 1970s.

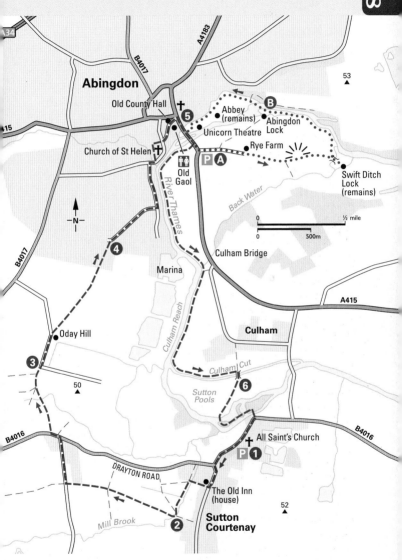

WALK 28 DIRECTIONS

1 From the car park go across to the B4016 and turn left, joining the adjacent tree-lined path.

Take the turning for Milton then, 25yds (23m) before the recreation ground road, take a narrow fenced path beside a house, The Old Inn. Cross a footbridge to some cottages and swing left to a kissing gate. Keep left at the immediate fork and follow the path alongside the Mill Brook. Cross a double stile and a footbridge and continue to the next stile and footbridge.

2 Turn right to walk nearly 0.75 mile (1.2km), initially on tarmac but then a broad track, narrowing to a path between hedges. At a road turn right, then left at the next junction, following Drayton Road. Take the second signposted right of way on the right.

WHILE YOU'RE THERE

Visit Abingdon Museum, which occupies the Old County Hall. As well as local archaeology and exhibitions, the museum houses the Southern Arts Craft Collection, which can be viewed by appointment. On Saturdays from April to September, the balconied roof is open to the public (small fee).

3 Keep ahead when the path joins a tarmac road and, when it curves left by a pair of cottages, look for a stile on the right. Go diagonally across the field, into the next pasture. Keep quite close to the left boundary and aim for some tall trees and houses in the distance. Veer right to the top right-hand corner of the field and find a footbridge with a handrail.

WHAT TO LOOK OUT FOR

The 12th to 14th century church at Sutton Courtenay is well worth a look. Herbert Asquith (1852–1928), British Liberal Prime Minister between 1908 and 1916, is buried in the churchyard, as is Eric Blair (1903–50), better known as George Orwell who, of course, wrote *Animal Farm* and *Nineteen Eighty-Four*.

WHERE TO EAT AND DRINK

Abingdon has a variety of pubs from which to choose, among them The Old Anchor Inn and the Broad Face. At Sutton Courtenay The George & Dragon and The Swan are both well-established.

Walk ahead with the field margin on your right. At the houses join a tarmac path. This is Overmead.

4 Follow Overmead, from number 31 counting down all the way to 1, to reach a T-junction. Turn right, passing Lambrick Way, to the next T-junction. Turn left and keep alongside the Thames to The Old Anchor Inn. Soon turn left through an archway by some almshouses. Keep the Church of St Helen on the right and head for the road. Cross over into East St Helen Street and make for the Old County Hall.

5 Turn right to reach Bridge Street, pass the Broad Face pub and cross the River Thames to the far bank. Go down the steps on the left to the tow path, pass under the road bridge and walk along the riverside path. Pass an illustrated map of Abingdon, go through a gate and cross meadows alongside the Thames, passing the ancient Culham Bridge on the left. Follow the line of Culham Reach and keep beside the water until you reach a sign for Sutton Courtenay.

6 Once over the cut follow the path across fields and back to the Thames. Cross several bridges and weirs at Sutton Pools and veer right at the road, passing The Wharf on the right. Follow the village street to the parish church and return to the car park.

A Stroll to Swift Ditch Lock

Extend the walk to a forgotten backwater of the Thames.

See map and information panel for Walk 28

DISTANCE 2.5 miles (4km) **MINIMUM TIME** 1hr

ASCENT/GRADIENT Negligible ▲▲▲ **LEVEL OF DIFFICULTY** ✦✦✦

WALK 29 DIRECTIONS (Walk 28 option)

Having passed the Broad Face pub on Walk 28, make for the car park on the far side of the river, Point **A**. Turn left and follow the tarmac drive towards Rye Farm. Pass Kingfisher Barn to reach some cottages and keep ahead, following the raised track across the fields. When the track eventually curves to the right, continue ahead by a line of trees. Glance back here for a good view of Abingdon church spire on the horizon. Make for a concrete bridge and keep right in the field.

Head for another bridge in the field corner and follow the path until you reach the site of the first Thames pound lock. The lock represented a significant leap forward in the way boats once travelled along the river. The remains of Swift Ditch Lock can just be seen in the trees. Walk alongside the lock to the point where you can see the Thames. Return to the footbridge in the field corner and go straight on along the boundary. Follow the tow path to Abingdon Lock, turn right and cross the weirs, where the river and the foaming water create a dramatic scene, Point **B**.

On the far side of the weirs, follow the path past a wooden footbridge on the right and alongside a stream for 600yds (549m). Cross over at the next footbridge, then turn left to walk through a car park. On the left is magnificent Cosener's House. About 100yds (91m) beyond this turn left into Checker Walk and, at the bottom, the wonderfully preserved 15th-century Maunciper's House is reached across a courtyard on the left. Here merchants, guests and travellers were housed by the abbey, while the maunciper, as housekeeper and almoner, saw to their needs.

In front of the Maunciper's House is the equally well-preserved Checker's or Exchequer's house, now known as the Unicorn Theatre. This very small, intimate theatre stages many amateur productions – everything from serious plays to restoration comedy. Inside is a chimney dating from the 13th century.

Follow the path through the arch alongside the right wall of the courtyard and cross Thames Street to see the mill wheel , which is still visible under the building of the Upper Reaches Hotel. Walk along Thames Street to rejoin Walk 28 in Bridge Street.

Memory Lane at Didcot

*Relive the past in two museums on this
delightful linear walk, returning by train.*

DISTANCE 5.25 miles (8.4km)) **MINIMUM TIME** 2hrs

ASCENT/GRADIENT Negligible ▲▲▲ **LEVEL OF DIFFICULTY** ✚✚✚

PATHS Urban walkway, clear field paths

LANDSCAPE Town outskirts and flat farmland

SUGGESTED MAP OS Explorer 170 Abingdon, Wantage

START/FINISH Grid reference: SU 525904

DOG FRIENDLINESS On lead on outskirts of Didcot, in Long Wittenham and Appleford. Under control in vicinity of Bow Bridge

PARKING Large car park at Didcot Parkway Station (none at Appleford)

PUBLIC TOILETS Didcot Parkway Station, Pendon Museum (for visitors)

WALK 30 DIRECTIONS

From the station forecourt turn left and pass Didcot Labour Club, then turn left at the junction 75yds (69m) beyond. Once through the railway tunnel, turn left (not half left) to join a tarmac path. Follow the path alongside the railway line, with the familiar chimneys of Didcot Power Station ahead of you on the horizon. Pass alongside modern housing estates, merge with another path and keep a footbridge on the left. Continue to a tunnel beneath the A4130 and leave the outskirts of Didcot, following the path along the field-edge.

Keep ahead between fence and stream and look for the outline of Wittenham Clumps (see Walk 43) on the far horizon over to the right. Make for a millennium mile post, one of 1,000 such posts to mark the creation of the National Cycle Network, and cross the road at Bow Bridge. Continue towards Long Wittenham, cross a bridge and swing away from the

water by a tongue of woodland. Keep on the path between fields and thick hedgerows and enter Long Wittenham. The tarmac path graduates to a lane before reaching Pendon Museum on the left.

Established on its present site in 1954, the museum reproduces, in miniature, scenes of the English countryside around 1930 – an evocative but accurate depiction of a bygone age. Exquisitely modelled cottages, farms, fields and chalky lanes recall the quiet charm of the Vale of White Horse. The museum houses many fascinating railway relics, as well as a reconstruction of a small Great Western Railway signal box. John Ahern's classic Madder Valley

---

WHAT TO LOOK OUT FOR

Didcot's huge coal-fired power station dominates much of this corner of Oxfordshire. The six cooling towers, built in the 1960s, are a very useful landmark for motorists and walkers.

Railway, dating from the 1930s, is on permanent display. This fascinating relic, which pioneered scenic craftsmanship, is operated on only five days a year because of its fragile condition.

Continue to the junction and war memorial and follow the main street. Pass The Plough and The Vine pubs and turn left by some thatched and timber-framed barns to reach St Mary's Church, cutting between two yew trees to the main door. Inside is a most impressive 12th-century font, made by casting two flat slabs of lead, embossed in the lower half with 30 figures of archbishops holding their right hands in benediction and their croziers in their left hands.

After visiting the church, return to the gate and swing right to join a footpath. Cross the churchyard to a kissing gate and follow the path as it curves behind the school and across rough grass to reach a drive. Turn left to the road, then turn right and retrace your steps to the war memorial. Keep ahead towards the museum and turn right immediately before a cottage (No 15).

Follow the track, keeping to the left of some gates, and emerge from some trees to skirt a field, hugging the right-hand boundary. You will soon be briefly reunited with the tranquil River Thames. Continue ahead in the field corner, cross a concrete footbridge and turn right to reach a wooden footbridge. Follow the path across the field towards trees and Appleford's church spire, just visible beyond. Make for a large oak on the far side of the field, pass into the next pasture and follow the path to the edge of Appleford. Make for the churchyard boundary, pass Manor Farm on the right and follow the road between houses. Keep right at the triangular junction and walk along to Appleford Station, from where frequent trains head back to Didcot Parkway.

When you get back, follow the signs for the Didcot Railway Centre, which, like the Pendon Museum, recalls the great days of steam travel. The site is operated by the Great Western Society, formed in 1961 and now one of the oldest preservation societies in Britain. The Didcot Railway Centre opened to the public in 1967, and a tour of the centre reveals the engine shed where visitors can see at first hand the magnificent collection of steam locomotives, many of them painstakingly restored over the years. A wide range of Great Western passenger coaches and a large assortment of vintage freight wagons can also be viewed.

A re-created country station is among the railway centre's many attractions, complete with its own level crossing and signal box. A unique Victorian signalling system can also be seen, as well as a faithful re-creation of Brunel's broad-gauge railway. The railway centre appears regularly on television and featured prominently in an *Inspector Morse* episode, *The Wolvercote Tongue*.

Thrupp's Christmas Eve Tragedy

Visit the scene of a 19th-century train crash on this gentle walk by the River Cherwell and the Oxford Canal.

WALK 31

DISTANCE 4 miles (6.4km)	MINIMUM TIME 1hr 30min

ASCENT/GRADIENT *Negligible* ▲▲▲   LEVEL OF DIFFICULTY ✚✚✚

PATHS *Field and waterside paths, canal tow path, 20 stiles*

LANDSCAPE *Level countryside with Oxford Canal and River Cherwell*

SUGGESTED MAP *OS Explorer 180 Oxford*

START/FINISH *Grid reference: SP 483159*

DOG FRIENDLINESS *Under control on tow path. On lead near livestock*

PARKING *Car park by maintenance yard at Thrupp*

PUBLIC TOILETS *None en route*

Sadly, British rail disasters continue to make the newspaper headlines at the start of the 21st century. But train crashes in this country are nothing new. As you reach the railway line in the closing stages of this very pleasant waterside walk, pause for a few moments and allow the imagination to picture what happened here more than 125 years ago.

Christmas Crisis

It was 1874, about noon on Christmas Eve, and there was heavy snow on the ground. A train from London's Paddington Station, bound for the Midlands, acquired an extra coach at Oxford to help cope with the large numbers of passengers travelling home for the festivities. As the train headed north out of Oxford towards Shipton-on-Cherwell Station, a wheel-tire (tyre) on the additional coach broke. Almost at once the final carriages left the rails. The rest of the train continued for some distance before plunging down the embankment beside the Oxford Canal. The proprietor of the nearby paper mill ran immediately to the scene of the crash. With the help of his workers and those passengers who had not sustained injury, he managed to convey the casualties to the manor house, the mill and other homes in the area. An Oxford surgeon, who had been visiting a patient at a nearby house, and a London doctor, travelling on the train, attended to the injured.

A Mission of Mercy

Some of the carriages slipped beneath the icy waters of the canal and with snow still falling and telegraph lines down, conditions that day could not have done more to hinder the rescue operation. However, word eventually reached Woodstock and Oxford and help was summoned. Even Lord Randolph Churchill, whose son Winston (see Walk 22) had been born just three weeks earlier, travelled over from nearby Blenheim Palace, bringing with him a supply of food and drink.

Today, we are used to the emergency services gearing swiftly into action when a disaster occurs. But in Victorian times, things moved at a much slower pace. A team of doctors eventually arrived by special train from

Oxford, bringing with them vital medical supplies. Fifty of the injured passengers were taken to the Radcliffe Infirmary in the city.

Thirty passengers died in the crash, regarded then as the worst in railway history, and more than 70 were injured. Queen Victoria sent a message of sympathy. For everyone involved, Christmas was a non-event that year. The Great Western Railway set up an inquiry and an inquest was opened on Boxing Day. The jury finally ruled that what happened was an accident prompted by adverse weather conditions which affected the wheel-tire.

Several recommendations were made and there was an urgent call for more safety precautions, as well as improved testing of communication cords. Lord Randolph Churchill wrote to *The Times* demanding a more effective breaking system for all express trains.

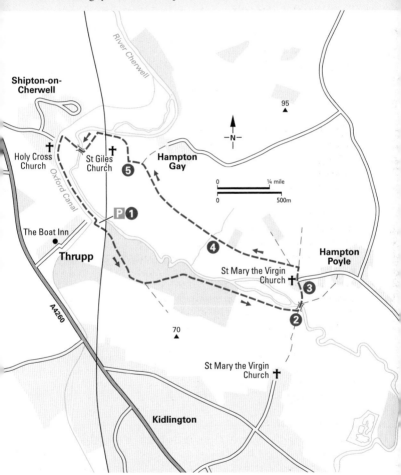

WALK 31 DIRECTIONS

❶ Leave the car park, walking back up the track, then turn left and pass to the right of cottages to go under the railway. Follow the

path through the plantation, keep left at the fork and head towards the bank of the Cherwell. The path stays quite close to the river. Eventually you emerge from the trees into an open field. The spire of Kidlington church can be seen to the right.

2 Draw level with the spire and look for a footbridge up ahead. Cross it to a stile and keep ahead in the field for about 50yds (46m) to a footbridge. Cross the field, aiming to the left of a bow-fronted house. Cross the next stile and go diagonally across the field to reach a stile leading out to the road.

3 Cross over to a stile, with Hampton Poyle's St Mary the Virgin Church seen here. Cross the pasture to a double stile, then keep to the left boundary in the field. After a few paces, look for two stiles in the hedgerow, avoid the path running extreme right and head diagonally right across a large paddock. Cross a stile in the corner, then aim half right to the top corner of the field.

4 Cross a stile and footbridge and go diagonally right across the field to a line of trees. Pass

over two wooden footbridges and a stile, then head out across the next field towards a gap in the hedgerow. Cross a stile here, heading towards the church at Hampton Gay and the remains of the manor house. Cross a stile and approach the house, veering left to the church.

5 Pass through a gate on your right just before the church and head diagonally across the field towards a railway bridge. Go through a gate by the river, pass under the railway to another gate and strike out across the field to a footbridge over the Cherwell. There are two stiles here. Cross the next field towards Shipton-on-Cherwell church and join a track just in front of it. Make for the Oxford Canal, cross a stile and drop down to the tow path. Turn left and walk back to Thrupp.

Garsington – Agriculture and Aristocracy

Pass a delightful manor house, which became a sanctuary for some famous writers and artists, on this undulating walk.

DISTANCE 3 miles (4.8km)   MINIMUM TIME 1hr 15min

ASCENT/GRADIENT 165ft (50m) ▲▲▲   LEVEL OF DIFFICULTY +++

PATHS Field paths and roads (can be busy in Garsington), 14 stiles

LANDSCAPE Rolling farmland to south-east of Oxford

SUGGESTED MAP OS Explorer 180 Oxford

START/FINISH Grid reference: SP 580024

DOG FRIENDLINESS Under control where requested and on lead in churchyard

PARKING Spaces near Red Lion in Garsington village

PUBLIC TOILETS None en route

For centuries the English village was the cornerstone of rural life. Farm labourers spent their money in the local shops and pubs and those who worked on the land or as servants in grand country houses were educated at the village school. People knew their place and didn't question it. They respected those who were seen as the pillars of the community – the landowner, the vicar and the doctor. They deferred to those above them.

The rural community is a very different place today, peopled by commuters, retired professionals and the self-employed. The class system still exists but in a very different form, and the local manor, once the domain of the local squire and a key component in the daily routine of the village, is now, in all probability, the home of a wealthy company director, a High Court Judge or a property developer.

Reminder of a Bygone Age

The manor house at Garsington is a typical example of what you might find in a traditional English village. The house is largely 16th-century and inside is an impressive staircase, various original stone fireplaces and some authentic 17th-century panelling. Near by is a 16th-century bakehouse and, beyond it, a 17th-century dovecote.

Graceful and imposing, the manor recalls a long-vanished world of style, elegance and good manners – a world inhabited by the well-heeled and the well-bred. Stand at the gate and you can picture the occupants of the house taking afternoon tea on the lawn during the summer or gathering at the front door to welcome guests as they arrived for a glittering weekend party. This would have been the scene at Garsington during the First World War and through the 1920s. At that time the manor house was the home of the noted society hostess Lady Ottoline Morrell, who died in 1938. Lady Ottoline, who was the sister of the Duke of Portland, married Philip Morrell, who represented the consituency of South Oxfordshire in Parliament and was also a member of the famous Oxford brewing family. Lady Ottoline and her husband invited many of the leading literary and

GARSINGTON

intellectual figures of the day to Garsington and soon it became a sanctuary for the likes of John Maynard Keynes, Virginia Woolf, T S Eliot and Bertrand Russell, among other members of the famous 'Bloomsbury Set'. Also part of this coterie were the English novelist and essayist Aldous Huxley and the poet Siegfried Sassoon. Huxley's most famous work had not yet been written when he visited Garsington. His *Brave New World*, written in 1932, is a disturbing portrayal of a Utopia peopled by human robots for whom happiness equals subordination. Sassoon used the manor as a refuge to try and rid his mind of the nightmare images provoked by his experiences as a serving soldier in the First World War.

It is now home to the Garsington Opera, founded in 1989 by Leonard and Rosalind Ingrams, with regular summer performances in a purpose-built auditorium on the terrace. The house is not open to the public.

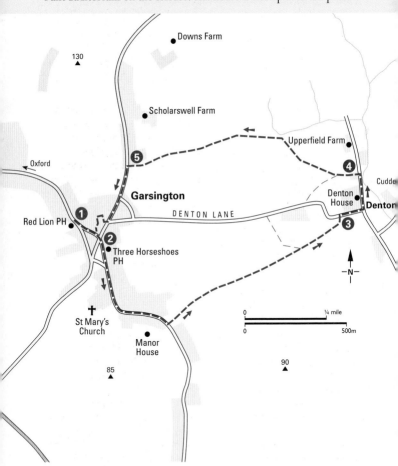

WALK 32 DIRECTIONS

1 Facing the Red Lion, turn left and walk through the village of Garsington. Veer half left at The Hill, leading to Sadlers

Croft. Keep right and climb the bank to some bollards by the war memorial. Cross over to The Green, keeping the Three Horseshoes on the left and an historic cross on the right.

2 Continue along the road to St Mary's Church and pass the Manor House. Keep on the road and, just as it descends quite steeply, branch left at a sign for Denton. Cross a stile and strike out across the field. Ahead on the horizon is the hilltop church at Cuddesdon, with a curtain of trees behind it. Make for a gap in the boundary and continue in the next field. Look for a waymark in a wide gap in the next boundary and aim to the right of a copse. Pass through the gap in the field corner, avoid the path on the left and head diagonally left across the field to the far corner. Cross two stiles to reach the road.

3 Turn right and pass alongside a stone wall on the left. Walk along to the right-hand bend and bear left at the sign 'Brookside only'. Imposing Denton House is on the left and a striking dovecote can be seen on the right. Pass a stile and footpath on the right and keep along the lane for a few paces, turning left at a public footpath.

4 Head for a stile and pass an ornamental wall enclosing Denton House. Cross a paddock to the next stile and then go diagonally right across the field to a stile. Then head diagonally left in the next field, keeping a farm over to the right. Cross two stiles and a plank bridge and begin approaching the houses of Garsington. Make for a stile in the right-hand corner of the field, keeping the boundary on your right in the next pasture. Climb gently and look for a stile on the right. Cross it, turn left and make for two stiles in the field corner. Join a drive and follow it up to the road.

5 Turn left towards Garsington, pass the houses of North Manor Estate and the village primary school before turning right, opposite Denton Lane, to join a footpath. Follow it to a lane, keep left and make for the road. Turn right and return to the parking area by the Red Lion.

Watlington – a Classic Small Town

Climb into spectacular Chiltern country and enjoy views towards a famous Civil War battleground.

DISTANCE 5.5 miles (8.8km)   **MINIMUM TIME** 2hrs

ASCENT/GRADIENT 200ft (60m) ▲▲▲   **LEVEL OF DIFFICULTY** ✦✦✦

PATHS Field paths and tracks, stretches of road (busy), 9 stiles

LANDSCAPE Level farmland and Chilterns escarpment

SUGGESTED MAP OS Explorer 171 Chiltern Hills West

START/FINISH Grid reference: SU 690943

DOG FRIENDLINESS On lead in Watlington, Watlington Hill and Watlington Park

PARKING Town car park in Watlington, on Hill Road (signposted, free)

PUBLIC TOILETS At far end of Watlington High Street

Standing at the foot of the Chilterns escarpment, close to the Icknield Way, Watlington is one of Oxfordshire's classic old towns – small and compact, and surrounded by some of the prettiest scenery to be found in the county. During the Civil War, Watlington stood in the shadow of battle, with opposing armies engaged in bitter conflict in the nearby fields.

Watlington's Town Hall

The quaint streets are lined with 17th-century half-timbered houses. Watlington's focal point is the gabled Town Hall, constructed in 1664. It is one of the oldest in the county. At one time a bridge connected the Town Hall to the upper floors of the nearby Hare and Hounds Hotel, now closed. The Town Hall was originally used as a a market hall, built with funds provided by one Thomas Stonor. The upper room was adapted for use as a Grammar School for boys until 1872, when a Board School was set up in premises in Davenport Place.

Another interesting building is Chiltern Gate, between the car park and Couching Street. It was opened by Lord Macclesfield in 1865 as a training school for those in domestic service. Up to 14 girls boarded here and were trained in cooking, housework and laundry. Lady Macclesfield paid some of the girls as little as six shillings per quarter.

The Missing Money Mystery

The original Hare and Hounds, which occupied a site near by, is associated with Colonel John Hampden, an MP and leader of the Parliamentary forces in the Civil War. He stayed at the inn the night before the Battle of Chalgrove Field in June 1643 and is alleged to have given the landlord, Robert Parslow, a chest containing money for the payment of troops. Hampden was fatally wounded in battle and never returned to Watlington. What happened to the chest is not known but some years later, perhaps driven by guilt, Parslow established a local charity to help the poor.

Watlington assumes the appearance of a small 18th-century market town, yet most of its streets were already complete by the 14th century.

WATLINGTON

During the 1730s the existence of about 260 houses was recorded. Today many of those buildings still recall their medieval origins – narrow on the street frontage but of considerable depth, with a side passage.

Wells and Watercress

The name of the town dates back to AD 880 when it was known as Watelingtone. Springs, wells and watercress beds add to its character and the chalk used as building material in the town's early development comes from pits at the foot of the Chilterns. The people of Watlington were given certain rights – including quarrying their own chalk for building houses. By the late 17th century Nettlebed (see Walk 35) bricks were in use, and tiles from the same Oxfordshire village began to replace thatch.

Medieval Settlement

To find the true heart of Watlington, walk along the High Street to New Road. This, reputedly, is the centre of the original settlement. During the 13th century a manor house stood on this site and the manor court was held here. The manor house later went into decline and the king's bailiff was accused of pilfering its timber and stone. The remains of a moat can still be identified in the churchyard.

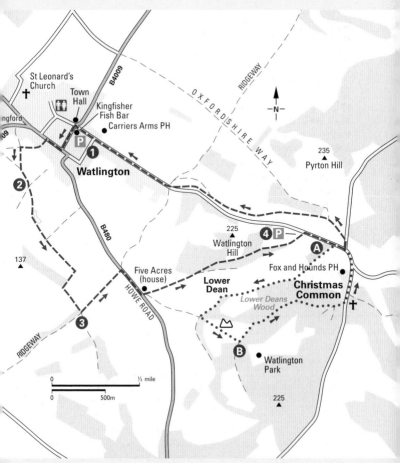

WALK 33 DIRECTIONS

1 Turn left out of the car park towards the town centre. Turn left at the junction, by the Town Hall, and follow Couching Street to the junction with Brook Street. Turn right and walk along to No 23. Take the footpath opposite and follow it between walls. Make for a kissing gate, keep right at the immediate fork and cross a field. Keep to the left of a tree and head for a second kissing gate, veering left at a possibly indistinct fork before it.

2 Turn left to walk with trees on your left. Swing left at a wide black metal gate. Walk on for a further 0.5 mile (800m), passing a pond and then rising very gently, until a concrete farm track. Reaching it, turn left to join a path along the field-edge. Keep the hedge and trees on the right and follow it to a stile in the corner.

3 Turn left here and walk along the Ridgeway to the road. Turn right towards Nettlebed and then take the first left turning. Follow the track for about 70yds (64m) and, when it forks at a wooden post and brick pillar, keep left and follow the enclosed path through the trees to two stiles. Continue on the path, climbing gently to a kissing gate. Keep left at the fork and keep climbing. Break cover from the trees and then enter woodland again. Go through a kissing gate and pass between beech trees to the next gate. Follow the path to the right of Watlington Hill car park and turn right at the road.

4 Head for Christmas Common and turn left at the next junction. Follow the road for about 50yds (46m) and turn left at the Oxfordshire Way sign. Cross a stile and keep along the field perimeter to a second (but disused) stile. Keep ahead for about 70yds (64m) to a stile and leave the Oxfordshire Way here. Follow the sunken path, looking for white arrows on the trees, and descend gradually for 0.75 mile (1.2km). At a chalk pit turn left then right, to walk parallel to your previous line. Reach a kissing gate and turn right at the road. Follow it for 0.5 mile (800m) back to the car park.

WALK 33

Christmas Common and a Civil War Truce

Climb to elegant parkland and visit a hamlet with an unusual history.

See map and information panel for Walk 33

DISTANCE 2.5 miles (4km) **MINIMUM TIME** 1hr 15min

ASCENT/GRADIENT 330ft (100m) ▲▲▲ **LEVEL OF DIFFICULTY** ✦✦✦

WALK 34 DIRECTIONS (Walk 33 option)

From the road to Christmas Common, turn right at a footpath sign, over a stile by some galvanised gates, Point **Ⓐ**, and, after a few paces, you reach a gate on the right. Don't go through it, instead take a gate beside it, to descend steadily through trees. Further down, the path runs along the edge of woodland before reaching the old farm outbuildings at Lower Dean. Join a track running ahead and pass a barn conversion on the left. When the track bends right, turn left through the trees and, in just a few paces, go up to the left to a gate (not the track marked 'Private'). Make for a stile ahead and then follow the field track up the steep slope towards Watlington Park.

Look for a stile ahead in the trees, cross it and swing left after several paces, Point **Ⓑ**. On your right you can see the outline of Watlington Park. Follow the path ahead through the woods, veering right at one point. Pass a National Trust sign for Lower Deans Wood and continue for some time between the trees before reaching a drive.

The National Trust was founded in 1895 by three visionary Victorians whose objective was to acquire sites of historic interest and natural beauty for the benefit of the nation. The Trust's first property was the 14th-century Clergy House at Alfriston in East Sussex, purchased in 1896 for the princely sum of £10. The Trust, which is an independent charity, has come a long way since those early pioneering days.

Turn left and make for the road. Turn left, pass the little Church of the Nativity, built in 1889, and walk through Christmas Common to the Fox and Hounds pub.

It is said that Christmas Common takes its name from a significant day in the Civil War. By Christmas 1643, the Parliamentarians held nearby Watlington, while the Royalists defended the ridge on which Christmas Common is located. On Christmas Day itself, a temporary truce was called and both armies supposedly met on this site during the festivities – hence the name. Thus, the season of goodwill passed peacefully.

Follow the road to the junction and then rejoin Walk 33 just 150yds (137m) beyond where you left it.

Wild Orchids at Warburg

Glorious scenery and a visit to a secluded nature reserve in the Chilterns.

DISTANCE 4 miles (6.4km)	**MINIMUM TIME** 1hr 45min

ASCENT/GRADIENT 150ft (46m) ▲▲▲   **LEVEL OF DIFFICULTY** ✦✦✦

PATHS *Tracks, field and woodland paths, 4 stiles*

LANDSCAPE *Mixture of rolling hills and wooded valleys*

SUGGESTED MAP *OS Explorer 171 Chiltern Hills West*

START/FINISH *Grid reference: SU 701867*

DOG FRIENDLINESS *On short lead at all times within reserve*

PARKING *Room to park in vicinity of Pudding Stones*

NOTE *Warburg Nature Reserve Visitor Centre*

WALK 35 DIRECTIONS

From the Pudding Stones (found at the eastern end of Nettlebed High Street) take the access road that eases away from the A4130, and follow it for about 600yds (549m). Keep left at a fork, signposted 'Magpies', and follow this for about 0.5 mile (800m). Near Soundess House continue ahead into the trees when the track swings left at a footpath sign for Russell's Water.

Soon you reach an information board at an entrance to the Warburg Nature Reserve. Further on, at a diagonal junction, veer right to continue through the trees into a dry valley, descending gently, and soon a curtain of trees rises up in front of you. Pass the picturesque, timber-framed Pages Farm on the left and turn left at the access road. Walk along to the Warburg Nature Reserve's Visitor Centre and car park opposite.

The reserve, a Site of Special Scientific Interest (SSSI) is a haven of woodland and grassland, which includes a wide variety of wildlife and a nature trail. Named after an Oxford botanist, the reserve lies either side of a dry, winding valley and the pooling of cold air along the valley floor means that from time to time very hard frosts strike this delightful, though remote, corner of the county.

Covering 262 acres (106ha) and acquired in 1967, Warburg is the largest reserve managed by the Berks, Bucks and Oxon Wildlife Trust (BBOWT). Its mix of partly ancient woodland, scrub and flower-rich grassland has helped to establish the site as a major visitor attraction in the area in recent years. Warburg is especially famous for its flora, with more than 450 species of plants recorded, including 15 wild

WHERE TO EAT AND DRINK

Nettlebed has the White Hart Hotel. In nearby Highmoor is The Dog and Duck. If you want to stop for refreshments midway round the walk, the Warburg Reserve has a picnic area.

WARBURG NATURE RESERVE

orchids. Forty kinds of butterfly have been spotted here too, as well as 450 moths and 950 fungi.

WHAT TO LOOK OUT FOR

The Pudding Stones, at the eastern end of the village street, are a mystery, though they survive as perfect examples of some of the most ancient works of primitive peoples.

Lizards, snakes, adders, doormice, moles, hares, deer, bats and badgers are also known to inhabit the reserve. If you have the time, call into the very informative visitor centre, sit in the adjoining bird hide and watch all manner of creatures visiting the pond. You could even extend the route by following the reserve's popular Wildlife Walk.

A number of trees within Warburg have been felled to create a graded interface between the grassy rides and the woodland. This produces one of the richest wildlife habitats here – attracting a wide variety of butterflies, including the dark green fritillary, the comma and the speckled wood. The felled trees leave spaces where sunlight can penetrate, with the remaining trees acting as windbreaks.

Much of the wildlife found at Warburg is struggling to survive generally throughout Britain. With increased pressure for more housing and changes in agricultural practices, the future of the countryside is under threat. Thankfully, Warburg acts as a sanctuary for wildlife – one of only a handful of sites in the country where such a rich collection of species still survives. The efforts of conservation volunteers are halting the decline of these precious plants and

creatures. It is hoped that many will spread beyond the boundaries of Warburg and return to the natural habitat of the countryside.

Resuming the walk, continue ahead along the track. After 0.75 mile (1.2km) pasture reappears on both sides. Go ahead between a line of trees and a fence. Veer left when a track joins from the right, to approach the outbuildings of Westwood Manor Farm. When perhaps 75yds (69m) before a farm gate turn left, over a stile, and go up the field slope to a stile in the trees on the right. Take the path through the woodland, climbing gently. Cross another stile and head straight across the field, looking for a stile up ahead.

Pass a pond in the garden of a house, keep close to the left boundary and join a track. Turn left and follow it through woodland. After 200yds (183m), as the track curves right, go straight on along a path through the trees. Then 100yds (91m) further, at a U-bend, turn left and climb gently. After 75yds (69m) cross a track and go half right (there is another white arrow here), then, after just 30yds (27m) more, reach a tree on the right with its trunk shaped like a Y; branch left on a less distinct path to soon find some dilapidated fencing. Keep this fencing to your left to emerge by double gates to join a drive. Keep left at the next junction then, at Nettlebed High Street turn left, passing the old bottle kiln, back to the start.

WHILE YOU'RE THERE

Have a look at one of Nettlebed's most famous landmarks, in a residential close near the village street. The village bottle kiln was restored in 1972.

Uffington's Galloping White Horse

Discover the legends and magic of one of Britain's greatest antiquities on this spectacular downland walk.

DISTANCE 7 miles (11.3km)   **MINIMUM TIME** 3hrs 45min

ASCENT/GRADIENT 720ft (219m) ▲▲▲   **LEVEL OF DIFFICULTY** +++

PATHS Ancient tracks and field paths, road (can be busy), 9 stiles

LANDSCAPE Vale of White Horse and exposed downland country on Oxfordshire/Berkshire border

SUGGESTED MAP OS Explorer 170 Abingdon, Wantage

START/FINISH Grid reference: SU 293865

DOG FRIENDLINESS Under control or on lead in vicinity of the Uffington White Horse and along Ridgeway

PARKING Large car park near Uffington White Horse

PUBLIC TOILETS None en route

High above the Oxfordshire countryside stands the chalk figure of a galloping horse. Shrouded in the mists of the past, this noted 856ft (261m) high landmark, 365ft (111m) long and 130ft (40m) tall, represents one of Britain's most famous antiquities.

Mysterious and Beautiful

The best time to see the horse is early on a summer's day or during the week in the middle of winter, when the crowds and the cars are scarce. It is then that the Uffington White Horse exudes its own peculiar air of mystery. Regarded as far and away the most beautiful of all the British chalk hill figures, the horse is formed from a chalk-filled trench and, contrary to popular belief, not etched into the natural chalk. Its design is stylised, with an elegant, slender body and a distinctive beaked jaw similar to those displayed on early Iron-Age coins. There have been countless theories over the years as to its age and exact purpose.

A medieval document records it as one of the wonders of Britain, along with Stonehenge, while some sources suggest it was cut some time during the 1st century AD. Others claim it was established to celebrate King Alfred's victory over the Danes at the Battle of Ashdown in AD 871. In more recent times, the age of the horse has been scientifically pinpointed by a series of archaeological digs and analysis of soil samples, indicating that it dates back almost 3,000 years, to the late Bronze Age or early Iron Age.

Unanswered Questions

The horse is not clearly appreciated other than from the air or from some distance away – which gives credence to the theory that the White Horse may have acted as a tribal banner or badge for the inhabitants of the Vale of White Horse below. What does it symbolise and why was this particular site chosen? There are no conclusive answers. Certainly the White Horse is closely associated with mythology. One legend claims that the figure is

UFFINGTON WHITE HORSE

St George's steed and that the flat-topped chalk outcrop below, known as Dragon Hill, is where St George slew the beast. A bare patch on the summit is supposed to mark where the dragon's blood was spilt.

Literary Inspiration

The Uffington White Horse has also attracted its fair share of literary figures. G K Chesterton (1874–1936), creator of the fictional detective-priest Father Brown, wrote about it in his *Ballad of the White Horse*, and Thomas Hughes (1822–96), who was born in Uffington, described the custom of scouring the horse, clearing it of grass and weeds, in *The Scouring of the White Horse*. It was Hughes who helped revive the tradition, which at one time attracted as many as 30,000 volunteers.

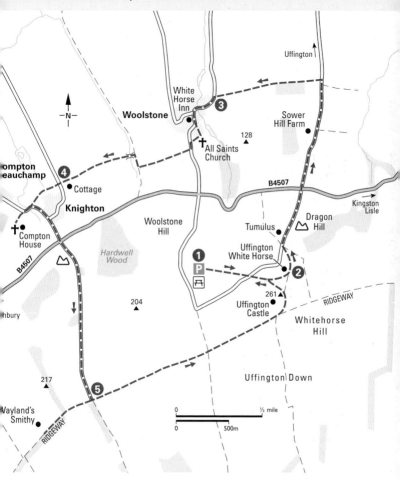

WALK 36 DIRECTIONS

1 From the car park go through any gate to follow the outline of the grassy path along the lower slopes towards the hill. Make for a gate and cross the lane to join a bridleway. Make sure to keep left at the fork, by a bridleway waymark, and walk along to the head of Uffington's galloping White Horse.

UFFINGTON WHITE HORSE

② Descend steeply on the path to the tarmac access road, keeping the chalk figure on your left. If you prefer to avoid the dramatic descent, retrace your steps to the lane, turn right and continue down to the junction with the B4507. Cross over and take the road towards Uffington, turning left at the path signposted to Woolstone. Go through a gate and keep the hedge on your right. Make for a stile in the field corner. Continue across the next field to a gap and cut through trees to the next gap. Keep ahead with the hedgerow on your left.

WHERE TO EAT AND DRINK

The White Horse Inn at Woolstone is on the route of the walk and serves food. Or try The Fox & Hounds at Uffington or the Blowing Stone at nearby Kingston Lisle which offers an extensive menu and a pleasant conservatory restaurant.

③ Through a kissing gate, turn left at the road and walk through the village of Woolstone. Turn left by the White Horse Inn and follow the road to All Saints' Church. At its metal kissing gate, veer right across the churchyard to a stile and gate. Cross a paddock to a further gate and stile. Turn left up the road for less than 100yds (91m) and turn right at the footpath sign. Walk for 0.25 mile (400m) with a hedge on your left side, across three fields, to a stile. Turn right and walk through the trees for about 150yds

(137m), looking for a concealed footbridge on your left. Cross the footbridge to a field, head diagonally left to a stile and turn right. Follow the field-edge to a stile and aim ahead, across further fields and stiles, to a thatched cottage. As you pass the cottage to your left you will reach a road.

④ Cross the road and follow the D'Arcy Dalton Way, signposted on the opposite side. Take a stile into a paddock then veer left, ascending slightly, to join a rough track to the road by the village sign for Compton Beauchamp. Cross over and take the drive to the church, next to the manor. Retrace your steps to the sign and walk up to meet the junction with the B4507. Cross over and climb quite steeply to the Ridgeway.

⑤ Turn right for 550yds (503m) if you wish to visit Wayland's Smithy (see While You're There). Otherwise, turn left and stride out for a long mile (1.6km), resisting a path into the Uffington Castle fort. At the highest point on the track, about 50yds (46m) beyond a track junction, turn left. Go to the trig pillar, then swing left (visiting the fort first) and descend to rejoin the outward track, back to the car park.

WHAT TO LOOK OUT FOR

All Saints' Church at Woolstone is a lovely chalk-built church. Inside you'll find a lead font and some striking 20th-century Stations of the Cross.

Visit Wayland's Smithy, just off the route. This impressive 5,000-year-old long barrow occupies a remote, ghostly setting. Crowning Whitehorse Hill is Uffington Castle, an Iron Age hill-fort situated high on the Ridgeway. The hill-fort covers abou 8 acres (3ha).

Stonor Park and a Secret Printing Press

Explore the rolling countryside of the Chiltern Hills before crossing a beautiful deer park.

DISTANCE 3.5 miles (5.7km) **MINIMUM TIME** 1hr 30min

ASCENT/GRADIENT 295ft (90m) ▲▲▲ **LEVEL OF DIFFICULTY** ✦✦✦

PATHS Wood and parkland paths and tracks, country lanes, 2 stiles

LANDSCAPE Spectacular Chilterns

SUGGESTED MAP OS Explorer 171 Chiltern Hills West

START/FINISH Grid reference: SU 735883

DOG FRIENDLINESS On lead through grazed areas

PARKING Off-road at southern end of Stonor, by barns of Upper Assendon Farm, which straddle road

PUBLIC TOILETS Stonor Park, for visitors; otherwise none en route

Without question, the chief attraction of this walk is Stonor, a mansion set in its own magnificent parkland amid the rolling Chilterns and open to the public at various times of the year. There has been a house here since the Norman Conquest – the core of the present one dates from the medieval period and has been enlarged and restored a great many times over the years.

The 18th-century façade of red brick encloses an E-shaped Elizabethan house with work dating from an earlier era behind it. Within its walls lies a maze of rooms and staircases, with sculptures, tapestries, drawings, paintings and many items of fine furniture on display.

Campion the Martyr

Stonor is also known for its 14th-century Chapel of the Holy Trinity, and it was here in 1580 that Lady Stonor gave refuge to the Jesuit priest and martyr Edmund Campion. Born in London in 1540, Campion was educated at Christ's Hospital in Sussex and St John's College, Oxford. He later became a deacon in the Church of England but fled to Douai in France when his Roman Catholic leanings became apparent. In 1573 he joined the Society of Jesus in Bohemia.

Campion became Professor of Rhetoric at Prague but returned to England in 1580 for a Jesuit mission. He preached in this part of the Chilterns and lived in secret at Stonor House, which at that time was a refuge for Catholics. The Stonor family was of the same faith and as a direct result of their religious devotion, endured persecution and imprisonment as well as the loss of many of their estates during the 16th and 17th centuries.

Here, using a printing press in a hidden room of the house, Campion supervised the printing of his book *Decem Rationes* (The ten reasons [for being a Catholic]), distributing 400 copies in St Mary's, Oxford, before the degree-giving ceremony in June 1581.

Trial and Execution

As a consequence of what he did, Campion was arrested, while preaching at Lyford in Berkshire. He was tried on a charge of conspiracy and, having refused to renounce his faith, was executed on 1 December. Before he was hanged, he wrote: 'If our religion do make us traitors we are worthy to be condemned, but otherwise we are and have been good subjects as ever the queen had.' Campion was beatified in 1886 and later canonised as one of the 40 Martyrs of England and Wales. His feast day is 25 October.

A visit to Stonor is certainly memorable, but a stroll through its glorious deer park and beechwoods makes a lasting impact — particularly on an autumn day when the leaves are beginning to turn.

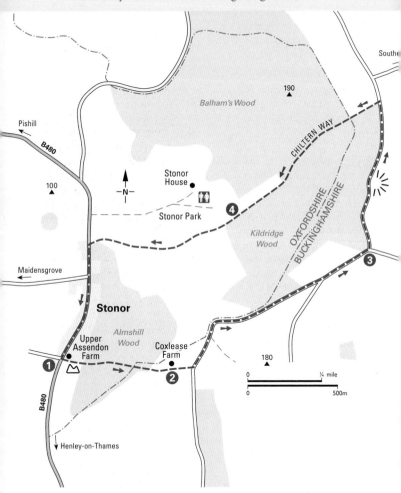

WALK 37 DIRECTIONS

❶ Cross the road to the 30mph speed restriction sign at the southern end of Stonor and turn left at the stile just beyond it to join a footpath. Keep the farm outbuildings on your left and go up the slope towards trees. Cross a stile into the woodland and begin climbing very steeply into the Chilterns. Look for the

STONOR

white arrows on tree trunks and further up you reach a clear track on a bend. Take this track, cross another and pass alongside Coxlease Farm.

2 Keep to the right of the outbuildings and join a track leading to the farmhouse. Make for the road and turn left. Follow this road for 0.75 mile (1.2km) as it passes several properties, bends sharp right, then curves left slightly. Next is a straight section which runs alongside Kildridge Wood, an area of mixed woodland and bracken, part of which has been recently harvested and replanted. Pass some double wooden gates on the right and keep to the road as it curves right. Turn left after a few paces, signposted towards Southend.

3 Keep Kildridge Wood on the left still, with views over fields and rolling countryside on the right. Follow the lane for 0.5 mile (800m) until you reach a turning on the left – the Chiltern Way. Follow the path beside a pair of brick and flint cottages, following the way towards Stonor Park. Cross a junction of tracks and descend between trees. Some of the trunks carry the CW symbol for Chiltern Way. Keep left at the fork, passing between laurel bushes and trees, and eventually you reach a deer fence and gate.

4 Pass alongside a tall wire fence and gradually Stonor (the house) edges into view. Head down towards the road and look for a kissing gate in the deer fence. Turn left and head for Stonor village. Pass a footpath and a turning to Maidensgrove and keep ahead to the former village pub. Continue through the village and return to the parking area.

Wallingford and William the Conqueror's Castle

Discover the ancient treasures of a famous town on the Thames before following a pretty stretch of river bank.

DISTANCE 3 miles (4.8km)	**MINIMUM TIME** 1hr 30min
ASCENT/GRADIENT Negligible ▲▲▲	**LEVEL OF DIFFICULTY** +++

PATHS Bridleways, pavements, Thames Path, 11 stiles

LANDSCAPE Flat farmland by Thames

SUGGESTED MAP OS Explorer 170 Abingdon, Wantage

START/FINISH Grid reference: SU 604895

DOG FRIENDLINESS Mostly on lead or under strict control; on short lead at nature reserve

PARKING Long-stay car park in St George's Road, Wallingford

PUBLIC TOILETS Off High Street in Wallingford

Wallingford is one of those towns that can hold your attention for hours. Its churches are well worth a look, its museum and Town Hall attract many visitors, and the grass-covered mounds of its ruined castle serve as a reminder of the bitter struggle for supremacy during the Civil War. Wallingford has even made guest appearances in television drama – most recently as the town of Cawston in the popular thriller series *Midsomer Murders*. Scenes were filmed in the Market Place.

A Royalist Stronghold

Turning the pages of history, you'll find Wallingford was once acknowledged as an important river crossing, and in the 11th century William the Conqueror deemed a large castle was necessary to protect it. William crossed the Thames here in 1066 and today the river is spanned by a splendid 900-ft (274m) bridge of 16 arches. The castle was the last Royalist stronghold in Oxfordshire to surrender, following a brave Parliamentary siege that lasted 65 days. Cromwell ordered it to be demolished six years later.

Elsewhere, there is much to see. The Town Hall is one of Wallingford's finest buildings. Resting on pillars, it houses the tourist information centre. Inside the Town Hall are portraits by Lawrence and Gainsborough, as well as a silver mace and the 15th-century town seal. In front of the building is a striking war memorial, unveiled in 1921.

Across the road is the 19th-century Corn Exchange, now a theatre. Look for the Victorian drinking fountain at the northern end of the Market Place, given to Wallingford by Alderman Hawkins.

Wallingford's Wonderful Churches

No visit to Wallingford is complete without a look at its churches (the town once had 16, but there are now only six). One of the most striking of these holy buildings is St Peter's Church with its needle-like spire. The church, which was rebuilt in 1769–77, contains the tomb of Sir William Blackstone

(1723–80), Oxford's first professor of English law, who presented St Peter's with a clock from Horse Guards in London.

Not far away, along Thames Street, and defining the south-east corner of the old Saxon walled town, is St Leonard's Church. The churchyard, which has been managed by a wildlife conservation group since 1996, is a haven for wildlife in an urban setting. To facilitate improved conservation, the churchyard has been divided into various areas, each with its own distinct environmental features. It's worth allowing time to stroll through the churchyard, which you pass towards the end of the walk, as it reveals a variety of habitats and wildlife surprises.

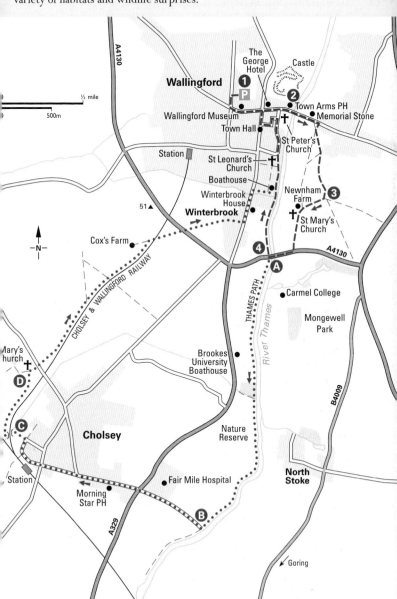

WALK 38 DIRECTIONS

1 On leaving the car park turn left and walk along St George's Road. Turn left into High Street and head towards Wallingford town centre. Pass the library and Wallingford Museum and keep ahead to the junction with St Martin's Street and Castle Street. The Town Hall is on the right and the remains of the castle on the left. Continue over the junction and pass Lamb Arcade and The George Hotel. On the right is the spire of St Peter's Church in Thames Street.

WHERE TO EAT AND DRINK

Wallingford has a choice of pubs, hotels and tea rooms from which to choose. The George Hotel and the Town Arms are directly on the route, while further afield, at Cholsey, is The Morning Star, offering basic meals and snacks.

2 Pass The Town Arms and cross the bridge over the Thames. Continue along the road and, about 80yds (73m) beyond the traffic-lights, turn right at a bridleway signposted 'Ridgeway and Grim's Ditch'. Follow the enclosed track between fences, keeping the river and adjacent meadows to your right. Keep left at a waymark and stay on the bridleway. Cross a footpath and now the woodland gives way to open fields.

3 On reaching a junction with a concrete farm track, turn right and head towards the buildings of Newnham Farm. Keep left and walk along the track to St Mary's Church at Newnham Murren. With the church on your right, continue on the tree-lined bridleway. Approaching the

A4130, veer right at the 'cyclists dismount' sign and follow the pavement along to a bridge over the Thames. Once over the bridge, veer right and follow the tarmac path down the bank to the riverside.

WHILE YOU'RE THERE

Wallingford Museum is housed in part of a medieval hall-house. One of its major attractions is a time-warp walk through Saxon and medieval Wallingford with personal audio commentary. Also on display are a Victorian shop, a pub and a model of Wallingford Station.

4 Turn left, soon fenced beside pastures then gardens, and passing a boathouse. The path becomes a tarmac drive between houses. Just 10yds (9m) beyond a property called The Boathouse turn right through an archway to the road by St Leonard's Church. Turn right for 400yds (366m), going through a 'no entry' sign and following 'Thames Path' signs to St Peter's Street, just before the main road. Turn left here, then left again into Wood Street. After 70yds (64m) turn right into a narrow alleyway called Mousey Lane and make for the Town Hall and the start.

WHAT TO LOOK OUT FOR

As you cross the River Thames at Wallingford, in the early stages of the walk, look down to your left and you'll spot a memorial stone which recalls that the field here was presented to the borough by Alderman and Mrs Lester in memory of their son, who was killed in action in 1944, aged 27.

Cholsey's Crime Queen

Visit the grave of a famous author on this pleasant spur to Cholsey.

See map and information panel for Walk 38

DISTANCE *8.75 miles (14.1km)*   **MINIMUM TIME** *3hrs 30min*

ASCENT/GRADIENT *Negligible* ▲▲▲   **LEVEL OF DIFFICULTY** +++

WALK 39 DIRECTIONS
(Walk 38 option)

Turn right and follow the Thames Path under the A4130 road bridge, Point **A**. Keep along the tow path, passing the buildings of Carmel College on the opposite bank. Go through a series of galvanised gates and Brookes University boathouse on the right. Cross fields and meadows and gradually the Fair Mile Hospital buildings edge into view. Enter Cholsey Marsh Nature Reserve and pass a seat by the river.

Turn right at a sign indicating a byway to Cholsey railway station, Point **B**. The track graduates to a lane before reaching the A329. Cross into Papist Way and pass The Morning Star (on left). Continue through Cholsey and cross Station Road into West End. Avoid the railway bridge and bridleway as the road curves right and head for Sandy Lane, Point **C**.

Turn left opposite it on an enclosed footpath, avoiding a footbridge on the right. Pass under the Cholsey and Wallingford railway and turn immediately right at a bridge over a stream. Walk alongside the railway to a footbridge and kissing gate.

Skirt the next field, heading towards the church. Make for the field corner where there is a footbridge and gate. Cross the field to the churchyard, Point **D**. To visit Agatha Christie's grave and its imposing headstone, keep to the left of the church and it will be found along the back wall.

Agatha Christie (1890–1976) lived at nearby Winterbrook House, having previously lived at Sunningdale in Berkshire. A prolific crime writer, she is probably best remembered for her play *The Mousetrap* – a classic whodunit – which has been performed in London over 23,000 times since 1952, and to date shows no sign of closing.

Make for the churchyard exit and cross the road to a stile. Go diagonally right across the field to a stile by the railway. Follow the line for some time, crossing eight stiles to reach a track crossing the railway. Veer right here and walk along to the A4130. Cross it to a stile and follow a grassy path between fields. Approach Winterbrook and turn left when you get to the road. Pass Winterbrook House as you follow Reading Road for 350yds (320m). Turn right, through a metal barrier on to a tarmac path to walk beside a tributary stream of the Thames and rejoin Walk 38 at the river bank.

Old Father Thames at Goring

Follow the tow path beside the Thames and return from Pangbourne by train.

DISTANCE 5 miles (8km) **MINIMUM TIME** 2hrs

ASCENT/GRADIENT 90ft (25m) ▲▲▲ **LEVEL OF DIFFICULTY** ✦✦✦

PATHS Tow path, field and woodland paths, village roads, no stiles

LANDSCAPE Thames Valley meadows and beechwoods

SUGGESTED MAP OS Explorer 171 Chiltern Hills West

START/FINISH Grid reference: SU 599806

DOG FRIENDLINESS Under control on Thames Path; on lead in villages

PARKING Station Road in Goring (or either train station)

PUBLIC TOILETS At car park and Pangbourne main car park

WALK 40 DIRECTIONS

From Station Road car park take the tarmac path beside the toilets. Turn left down the High Street, passing The Miller of Mansfield pub and the village hall, dated 1925. Look for the Thames Path sign and join the tow path.

The end of Ferry Lane, over on the left, represents the point where the Ridgeway and the Icknield Way once crossed the river at a ford. Both paths originally formed a prehistoric trade route between Dorset and East Anglia. The ford was important to the Romans and resulted in a raised causeway here. Settlements were established by the crossing and in Anglo-Saxon times the river became a vital frontier. Streatley, over on the Berkshire bank, was part of Wessex, while Goring was in Mercia.

Head downstream with the river on your right. Follow the trail, first by the water's edge, passing boathouses in various states

of repair. Later the path skirts meadows and fields, on its way to Gatehampton. There used to be a ferry here, one of many services along the entire length of the Thames, but most of them were discontinued during the Second World War.

The Thames is historically the most important river in Britain, used as a highway since early times. To stroll along its banks is the only way to appreciate its unique beauty and character. The 180-mile (290km) Thames Path, officially opened in July 1996 by the Countryside Commission (now the Countryside Agency), is the only long distance national trail in the country to follow a river for its entire length. Over 13 million people live within its catchment area and with numerous access points, frequent public transport services, a high standard of waymarking and many points of interest, the Countryside Agency believes its long-term popularity is assured.

The user-friendly terrain and level, easy-going surface enable walkers to tackle the route at any time of year, though stretches of the river bank can become wet and muddy after prolonged rain. More than 95 per cent of the trail currently follows the intended route, running beside the river, which begins life as a trickling stream in a Gloucestershire field near Cirencester.

Despite problems over access in several places, the Thames Path has come a long way since the 1920s when the concept of providing public access along the length of the river was first mooted. Over the years, increasing public demand for recreation and access to the countryside led to the eventual designation of the route in 1989. Much of the Thames Path is set against an urban background but, even here, there are many distinguished buildings and famous monuments to be seen, reflecting Britain's history and tradition.

Between Wallingford and Reading, the Thames is most closely associated with the 'Goring Gap' where, during the ice age, the river carved a new passage through the chalk hills, cutting between the Berkshire Downs and the Chilterns.

A pill box, a reminder of the dark days of 1940 when Britain faced a very real threat of invasion, is passed as you follow the trail beneath Brunel's original Paddington-to-Bristol railway line. Pass through several galvanised gates and walk along to a gate for Ferry Cottage. At this point turn left, away from the river bank. On reaching a T-junction, turn right and follow the path parallel to the Thames, cutting between the trees of Hartslock Wood. Look for another pill box down to your right, partly concealed by woodland, and keep ahead. The river is glimpsed between the trees as you climb above it.

After 0.75 mile (1.2km) emerge from the woodland and continue between fields. Descend a flight of wooden steps then climb another, and keep ahead on a drive for a long 0.5 mile (800m), passing Elm Cottage and Coombe Park Farm. Turn right at the road, following it down into Whitchurch village. Pass Manor Road, The Greyhound pub and the Ferryboat Inn before reaching the toll house.

Cross the Thames to the Adventure Dolphin Centre at Pangbourne on the Berkshire bank, then turn right by the Boathouse surgery and follow the waymarked footpath to the road. Opposite is Pangbourne railway station.

At Goring station cross the bridge over the high speed tracks to the pedestrian exit: this leads to Station Road. Follow it for 250yds (229m). Turn right to the start.

WHAT TO LOOK OUT FOR

Whitchurch Bridge is a Victorian toll bridge distinguished by its white lattice architecture. Motorists pay to cross the bridge but pedestrians go free. The bridge is privately owned.

Buscot to Kelmscott

On the Thames Path to the home of William Morris.

DISTANCE 4.75 miles (7.7km)		**MINIMUM TIME** 2hrs	

ASCENT/GRADIENT 82ft (25m) ▲▲▲   **LEVEL OF DIFFICULTY** ✦✦✦

PATHS *Riverside paths, fields, village lanes, 6 stiles*

LANDSCAPE *Open, flat lands of the Thames floodplain*

SUGGESTED MAP *OS Explorer 170 Abingdon, Wantage & Vale of White Horse*

START / FINISH *Grid reference: SU 231976*

DOG FRIENDLINESS *On lead around weir, not permitted in Manor gardens*

PARKING *National Trust car park (free) in Buscot, signed 'Buscot Weir'*

PUBLIC TOILETS *Buscot, behind phone box*

The village of Kelmscott is famous for its connections with the founder of the Arts and Crafts Movement, William Morris (1834–96). Today he is best remembered for his furnishing designs, rich with flowers, leaves and birds, still popular on fabric and wallpaper.

Champion of Fine Craftsmanship

Throughout his life, working with great Pre-Raphaelite artists such as Edward Burne-Jones and Dante Gabriel Rossetti, Morris dedicated himself to a movement against what he saw as the vulgar tastes of his day, with its sentimentality, clutter and gewgaws. He put a new value on craftsmanship, studying and experimenting with the techniques of ages past, and so developing a style of apparent simplicity combined with functionality. He took it upon himself to educate as well as create, with pronouncements such as 'Have nothing in your houses that you do not know to be useful, or believe to be beautiful' emphasising the place of good design in everyday life. His philosophy of design became hugely influential.

Morris looked to the medieval artists and architects for his inspiration – a favourite outing for visitors to Kelmscott was to the magnificent Great Barn, a medieval stone-built tithe barn at nearby Great Coxwell (now cared for by the National Trust), to admire the intricacies and craftsmanship of its soaring timber roof.

Manor and Village

Kelmscott Manor itself dates from 1570 and became Morris's country home in 1871. It's a mellow old place, built of the local grey limestone, with mullioned windows and high pointed gables topped by ball finials. (The image is familiar from the woodcut designed for the Kelmscott Press, which he founded in 1890.) Morris loved the manor for its integrity and austerity, and for the harmony of the house in its setting, almost as if 'it had grown up out of the soil'. Now owned by the Society of Antiquaries of London, the house is open to the public on Wednesdays and some Saturdays through the summer, and contains many examples of Morris's work.

BUSCOT

William Morris's influence on the area continued even after his death. As a memorial to the great man, several structures were designed to his principles and built in Kelmscott village, notably Memorial Cottages and next-door Manor Cottages. On a wider scale, Morris's work did much for the emergence of a Cotswold identity in the 1920s, with his appreciation and publicising of the vernacular architecture.

Morris is buried with his wife and daughters in the churchyard at Kelmscott, under a modest tombstone.

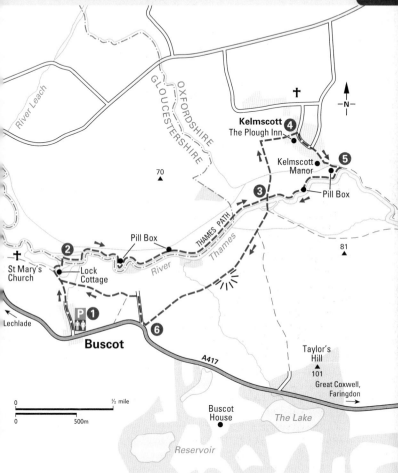

WALK 41 DIRECTIONS

1 Turn left and walk back into Buscot to admire the arcaded pump. Retrace your steps and continue ahead on the road, signed to the weir. Follow the road past the Village Field. Keep right down a path to pass Lock Cottage. Follow the footpath over a weir. Then bear left and cross the lock gate.

2 Turn right immediately, pass the lock, go through a gate and follow the path beside the river. Soon bear left through a gate and cross a bridge, with a view left to the main weir. Turn right and follow the Thames Path beside the meandering river. Go through two gates, and continue past two wartime pill boxes and a gate. Go through a pair of gates. The roofs of Kelmscott appear ahead. Go through a gate and continue towards the bridge, passing through some trees.

3 Pass the bridge, go through a gate and turn left through a squeeze stile up the field. At the far side cross a stile and two footbridges. Bear left and ahead up the hedge (yellow waymarker). At the end turn right along the path, which may be overgrown. Follow this into Kelmscott village.

4 Turn right to pass The Plough Inn. Bear left along the road, passing Memorial Cottages and Manor Cottages. Keep right to reach Kelmscott Manor. Maintain your direction ahead down the track and turn right just before you get to the river.

5 Cross a bridge and go through a gate to join the Thames Path National Trail. Go through a

gateway and continue, passing another old wartime pill box on your right. Go through the gate by the footbridge and turn left over the bridge. Bear left and right over another bridge. Cross a stile and walk up the track. Soon this crosses a ditch; now head diagonally right across the field. At the corner cross a stile and footbridge by the fingerpost and turn right. Keep straight on up the edge of the field, with views of Buscot House, left. Follow the track downhill, and bend right, then turn left over a footbridge. Continue on the path diagonally right across the next two fields.

6 Go through a gate by the road and turn right up a drive. Look out for a yellow waymarker and take the footpath off to the left. Soon cross a stile and veer left along the edge of the field. Cross a stile and a footbridge at the other end, walk across the Village Field and turn left to retrace your route back to your car at the start of the walk in Buscot.

Opposite: The gardens surrounding Kelmscott Manor

Mysteries at Minster Lovell

A gentle stroll through meadows and woods beside the Windrush.

DISTANCE *4 miles (6.4km)*   MINIMUM TIME *1hr 30min*

ASCENT/GRADIENT *180ft (55m)* ▲▲▲   LEVEL OF DIFFICULTY ✦✦✦

PATHS *Meadows, tracks, pavement and lane, woodland, 2 stiles*

LANDSCAPE *Shallow, fertile valley of River Windrush*

SUGGESTED MAP *OS Explorer 180 Oxford, Witney & Woodstock*

START / FINISH *Grid reference: SP 323114*

DOG FRIENDLINESS *Lead essential on road through Crawley and Minster Lovell*

PARKING *Car park (free) at eastern end of Minster Lovell village, above church and hall*

PUBLIC TOILETS *None en route*

Crawley's industrial heart is announced by its tall mill chimney, which dominates the shallow, verdant valley to the north of Witney. By comparison, a mile or two to the west, old Minster Lovell is the essence of an idealised Cotswold village. Its little houses of grey-brown stone straggle up a narrow street, adorned with impossibly pretty cottage gardens. At the top is a golden stone church, looking down over a silvery meander of the River Windrush. At the bottom is a lovely old pub, the Swan, with the former mill opposite now restored and part of a conference centre.

Two villages appeared on the site in the Domesday Book – Minster Lovell and Little Minster, separated by the river. There's now a newer Minster Lovell to the south-west, an experimental housing and allotment development dating back to the 1840s.

No perfect Cotswold village would be complete without its manor house, of course. And Minster Lovell's is a beauty, although in ruins. The site, in a curve of the river below the church, was picked out by Lord William Lovell, 7th Baron of Tichmarsh, in the 1440s. William's son John extended the new manor house, and signboards among the broken walls show how splendid it must have been, complete with a massive gatehouse.

A Gruesome Tale

William's grandson, Francis, was politically the most successful member of the family, but came to a nasty end. Raised as a Yorkist, he served as Lord Chamberlain to Richard III and fought with him at Bosworth Field in 1485. The King died in the battle and Francis took refuge in Flanders. Two years later he returned to take part in the Lambert Simnel rebellion, which backed an Oxford baker's boy for the throne. On the losing side in a battle at Stoke in 1487, Lovell fled home and was never heard of again. However in 1708, while a new chimney was being built at Minster Lovell Hall, it is said that a locked vault was discovered. In it was the skeleton of the missing Viscount Lovell, sitting with his papers at a table. Exposed to the air, the

MINSTER LOVELL

corpse dissolved into a cloud of dust in an instant. It was assumed that he had hidden here with the help of a servant, who subsequently fell ill and died, leaving unknown the secret of his master's whereabouts. John Buchan made chilling use of the legend in his novel *The Blanket of the Dark* (1931).

A pioneer of modernised agricultural techniques, Thomas Coke was the last resident at the Hall. He left in 1747 for his new Norfolk home, Holkham Hall. The ruins of the Hall are now cared for by English Heritage.

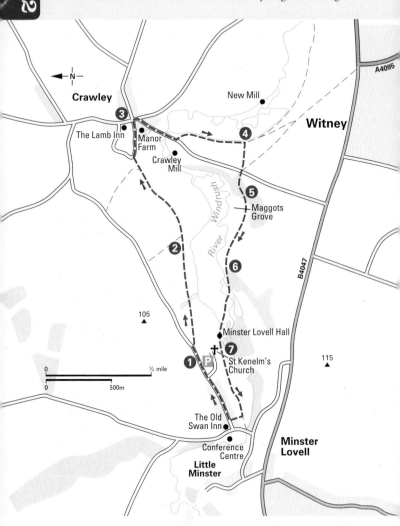

WALK 42 DIRECTIONS

1 Walk up the lane, signposted 'Crawley'. At the end of the village go through a gate, right, and take the footpath diagonally left across the field, also signposted 'Crawley'. Look right

for a view of the ruins of Minster Lovell Hall and the circular dovecote. Go through a gate near a field gate and continue straight on along the path, with a stone wall to your left. The mill chimney ahead on the horizon belongs to Crawley Mill.

MINSTER LOVELL

❷ Go through a gate and ahead up a slight incline. Cross two stiles and continue on the path, walking up a green tunnel of a lane. Pass above Crawley Mill. At the road turn right and follow this down into Crawley. At the bottom look left to admire the diminutive village green with its stone cross. The Lamb Inn is on the left.

❸ Turn right and follow the pavement past Manor Farm, with its huge pond. Cross the humpback bridge over the Windrush – look right for a good view of the old mill house. At the other side of the bridge cross the road and turn left through a gate, signed 'Witney'. Follow the bridleway beside the stream, marked by a line of willows.

❹ At the junction of paths by a gate look ahead and left to see New Mill. Turn right through the gate and walk up the field-edge. Pass a gate and cross the road. Go through the gate and straight on to a second gate, and follow the path down through the woods.

❺ At the bottom go through a gate and follow the path along the fence. The wildflower meadows of Maggots Grove lie to your right. Continue through four more gates and bear left beside the trees.

❻ Go through a gate and enter the woods. At a wooden gate bear right, following the arrows, and cross two footbridges. Continue on the path and cross a bridge over the river. Walk up the meadow towards Minster Lovell Hall. Go through two gates to explore the ruins.

❼ Leave by the top entrance and walk through the churchyard. Cross a slab stile, continue along a grassy path with the village up to your right. Cross a footbridge, go through a gate and veer to the right. Go through a gate and then another into Wash Meadow recreation ground. Keep right and go through a gate on to the high street, with The Old Swan pub to your left. Turn right and walk up through the village to the car park.

Dorchester – City to Commuter Village

Soak up the atmosphere of an ancient settlement before climbing to an outstanding viewpoint above the Thames.

DISTANCE 4.75 miles (7.7km)   MINIMUM TIME 2hrs

ASCENT/GRADIENT 115ft (35m) ▲▲▲   LEVEL OF DIFFICULTY ✦✦✦

PATHS Field and woodland paths and tracks, stretch of Thames Path and main road with pavement

LANDSCAPE Thames Valley

SUGGESTED MAP OS Explorer 170 Abingdon, Wantage

START/FINISH Grid reference: SU 578939

DOG FRIENDLINESS Under control in vicinity of Day's Lock and at Little Wittenham Nature Reserve; on lead near livestock

PARKING Parking area in Bridge End at southern end of Dorchester

PUBLIC TOILETS At parking area

Dorchester is steeped in history. On the surface it seems to represent the quintessential English village, inhabited by commuters and retired professionals. But there is much more to it than quaint winding streets and rows of chocolate-box cottages. The Romans built an important town here, Dorocina, though its ramparts are now only faintly recognisable, and the present abbey stands on the site of the first Saxon cathedral in Wessex.

Excavations have revealed a number of Roman artefacts in the locality – among them an altar to Jupiter and Augustus, various tessellated pavements and some Roman coins. Who knows what other relics of their occupation may lie beneath surface.

A Very Special Abbey

In effect, Dorchester is one of our oldest cities, though it seems hard to believe looking at it today. In 1140 the Bishop of Lincoln founded a priory here, endowing it with various valuable possessions of the bishopric. As a result, the cathedral became Dorchester's abbey church. Thankfully, it was saved from demolition at the time of the Dissolution and purchased by a local resident for the modest sum of £140. He bequeathed the abbey church to the parish of Dorchester in his will.

The abbey remains at the heart of Dorchester and is a very special place in the history of Christianity in this country. Inside are many treasures that illustrate the abbey's long and distinguished history. The 12th-century lead font is decorated with figures of 11 apostles seated beneath a striking Romanesque arcade. The nave is thought to have been built over the remains of the original cathedral and the east window is defined by a line of small sculptured figures depicting scenes from the life of Christ. Most of the glass in the top three rows dates from the early 14th century.

The Jesse Window has 14th-century tracery, sculpture and stained glass bound together in one single theme. It depicts the story of how Christ was descended from King David's ancestor Jesse.

DORCHESTER

The Right Revd Robert Runcie, Archbishop of Canterbury 1980–91, described Dorchester Abbey as 'a building which keeps alive our sense of the sacred in a busy world', while John Betjeman said it was 'splendid in its proportions and details.'

Saving the Abbey

A building of this size and importance does not come without its costs: between 1998 and 2006 some £4 million was spent on repair and refurbishment. Tasks included re-tiling three quarters of the roof, installation of central heating, repair of the chancel floor and the chancel wall sconces, and restoration and uncovering of some medieval wall paintings – all the more reason to allow yourself time to visit the abbey.

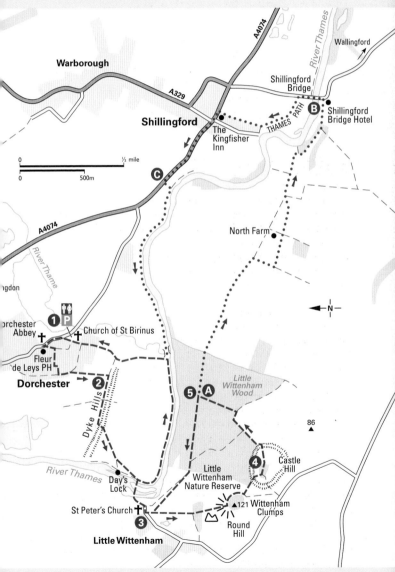

WALK 43 DIRECTIONS

1 From the parking area walk towards the centre of Dorchester, keeping the abbey church on the right. As you approach the Fleur de Les, turn left into Rotten Row and walk along to Mayflower Cottage and Pilgrims. Here turn right to walk beside allotments. Go forward and, on reaching a row of cottages, veer left to reach a road. Turn left but, after 60yds (55m), turn right at the sign for Day's Lock. Pass between fencing and out across a large field. Ahead is the outline of Wittenham Clumps. On reaching the low embankment of the Dyke Hills, turn right in front of the fence.

2 Follow the path along the field-edge, pass over a track and continue ahead. The path, enclosed by hedge and fencing, heads south-west towards the Thames river bank. Go through a gate towards Day's Lock but veer 175yds (160m) left of and beyond it, to a footbridge, Little Wittenham Bridge. Cross the river to Lock House Island and head for St Peter's Church at Little Wittenham.

3 Turn left just beyond it, at the entrance to the manor. Keep right at the immediate fork, go through a galvanised gate and begin a steep climb to the viewpoint and beech trees on Round Hill at the top. Veer left as you approach a seat, pass more seats and soon fork left, down to a gate at the foot of Castle Hill. Go through a galvanised gate, up a flight of steps and into the trees. On reaching a T-junction, turn left.

4 Emerge from the trees and pass a commemorative stone, keeping it on your right. Go down the grassy slope to a gate and pass through the trees to a field. Keep ahead along the perimeter, with woodland on the left. Pass a gate, continue along the field edge and swing round to the right at the corner but shortly turn left (not ahead with a waymarker) to join a nature trail and follow it through Little Wittenham Wood.

5 After 300yds (274m), at a T-junction with a wooden seat beyond it (Point **A** on Walk 44), turn left and follow the path back to Little Wittenham, forking right at a gate out of the woods after 600yds (549m). Recross the Thames and then turn right to follow the river downstream. On reaching the confluence of the Thames and the Thame (Walk 44 ends here), swing left before the footbridge and head north towards Dorchester. As the Thame bends right, go straight on to a kissing gate. Keep to the right of Dyke Hills to another gate and skirt the field to a track (Wittenham Lane). Pass the Catholic Church of St Birinus and return to the car park.

A Spur to Shillingford

Extend the walk by following a pretty stretch of the Thames.

See map and information panel for Walk 43

DISTANCE *7 miles (11.3km)* **MINIMUM TIME** *3hrs*
ASCENT/GRADIENT *Negligible* ▲▲▲ **LEVEL OF DIFFICULTY** ✦✦✦

WALK 44 DIRECTIONS
(Walk 43 option)

Turn right at the T-junction in Little Wittenham Wood, Point **A**, to break cover after 350yds (320m). Continue along the edge of the field, maintaining the same direction for 0.5 mile (800m) to reach a long-established 'diversion' around North Farm. Here turn right for 200yds (183m), then left, on a well-waymarked and fenced path. About 600yds (549m) on, cross the access road to North Farm from Shillingford obliquely, again well-waymarked. At a green metal gate go right, through woodland, ascending to that road (but go left if you would prefer to follow the river). Follow it towards Shillingford's classical bridge.

This reach of the river offers some of the finest scenery to be seen on the entire journey. The bank and surrounding countryside have always been very popular with tourists, cyclists and walkers. Built in 1827, balustraded and with three arches, Shillingford Bridge was originally built to carry the Wallingford to Thame turnpike over the river. The stretch of road here was turnpiked in 1764.

Walk through the car park of the Shillingford Bridge Hotel, Point **B**, to reach the road. Turn left to cross the bridge and then swing left, following the Thames Path sign. When the track bears left, veer right by the entrance to High Trees. Go through a gate and follow the path between fencing.

Cross the entrance to Shillingford Court – it was here in 1809 that the Thames rose to such a height that it was above head level. Walk down to rejoin the track, following it towards Shillingford. Keep ahead to the main road and turn left. Pass The Kingfisher Inn and follow the A4074.

On reaching a sign for Berinsfield and Dorchester, just before the road becomes a dual carriageway, cross over to a Thames Path sign and a kissing gate, Point **C**. Go straight down the meadow to reach the riverside path, keeping the Thames on your left now. The point at which you reach the river represents the site of Keen Edge Ferry, one of the original ferry crossings on the Thames. Cross the River Thame at the bridge and here rejoin Walk 43.

Blewbury's Bleak Downland

Savour the stillness and solitude of Oxfordshire's racing country.

DISTANCE *7.5 miles (12.1km)* MINIMUM TIME *2hrs 45min*

ASCENT/GRADIENT *360ft (110m)* ▲▲▲ LEVEL OF DIFFICULTY ✦✦✦

PATHS *Downland paths, concrete farm roads and wide tracks*

LANDSCAPE *Breezy open downland on Oxfordshire/Berkshire borders*

SUGGESTED MAP *OS Explorer 170 Abingdon, Wantage*

START *Grid reference: SU 532855*

DOG FRIENDLINESS *On lead in and near Blewbury; under control by gallops*

PARKING *Spaces in village, off A417*

PUBLIC TOILETS *None en route*

WALK 45 DIRECTIONS

From the illustrated map of the village on the main A417, veer off to the right by a seat and follow the path to the springs. Walk along to an information board and turn right here, passing alongside one of Blewbury's picturesque thatched cob walls. Go ahead towards the church but turn left in front of it and approach the village almshouses. Keep left here and take the little path. Veer left at the fork, cross a path and stream and then cut between the historic cob walls.

Join the road by The Red Lion and go straight on to the village war memorial, returning to the A417. Turn right. Opposite Westbrook Street turn left at the bridleway sign for the Ridgeway. Head south-west on the path, initially tree-lined, then by field-edge, passing seats as you ascend. After 1.5 miles (2.4km) you will reach a barn at Churn Farm. Turn right here, joining a concrete farm road. Pass brick and flint houses and turn left at the next junction.

Walk along to the next junction and ahead of you lies an old railway bridge. Turn left by Park Cottage and follow the concrete track straight and true for nearly 0.75 mile (1.2km). Where it curves left at a barred gate go straight on alongside a hedgerow. Follow this broad, rutted track for 700yds (640m), to join the Ridgeway at a signpost.

Britain's oldest road, the Ridgeway extends for 85 miles (137km) through the Buckinghamshire Chilterns to the Thames and then across Berkshire to touch Oxfordshire's southern boundary before reaching Wiltshire. In places the trail is as wide as a main road or a dual carriageway. When the original line became weathered or difficult to negotiate, travellers moved from one side to the other, gradually making the track wider. The character of the Ridgeway changes the further west you travel.

Initially, the trail cuts through gentle beechwood scenery and across soft rolling hills, but once across the Thames the Ridgeway cuts across bleak, exposed downland, offering little if any shelter from rain or wind. Take a moment to savour the stillness of this magnificent downland country. It is hard to imagine being more remote or cut off from civilisation than here in this quiet, rural backwater. At times, it can be quite uncanny.

Go ahead, but within 150yds (137m) fork left, away from the Ridgeway. Look for a motor vehicles sign at a crossroads. Turn left, cut between racing gallops, following the track with good views over to the right towards the Thames Valley and the familiar Wittenham Clumps (see Walk 43).

This part of Oxfordshire is synonymous with racehorse training. Racing as we know it today has its origins in the period of the Stuart kings. James I established stables at Newmarket and it was here that he kept racehorses and 'riders for the races' – the first royal jockeys. Towards the end of the 17th century, racehorses were beginning to appear all over the country, with many breeders introducing Arabian stock. Three of these stallions were the sires from which all our thoroughbreds are descended. As the sport began to draw spectator interest, it split into two different categories – flat racing and racing over jumps.

Underneath the grassland of the Berkshire Downs (embracing part of Oxfordshire) lies a flinty chalk soil. This was considered unsuitable for ploughing yet ideal terrain, once gallops had been set out, for racehorses and jockeys alike. These gallops, and training stables for racehorses, were soon a permanent feature of local country life.

When 75yds (69m) beyond the buildings of Whiteshoot Stables take the footpath, left. As you cross this field there is a view of your route. Descend through Lid's Bottom, a county wildlife site, and horse paddocks. Finally a path through trees strikes the A417 between the Barley Mow and the illustrated map in Blewbury.

Jarn Mound – a Wild Garden and a View

Discover how a local archaeologist moved the earth to protect a fine view of Oxford's famous skyline.

DISTANCE 5 miles (8km)	**MINIMUM TIME** 2hrs 15min

ASCENT/GRADIENT 150ft (46m) ▲▲▲   **LEVEL OF DIFFICULTY** ✦✦✦

PATHS Field paths and tracks, roads (can be busy), 11 stiles

LANDSCAPE Hilly, well-wooded country south west of Oxford

SUGGESTED MAP OS Explorer 180 Oxford

START/FINISH Grid reference: SP 495005

DOG FRIENDLINESS On lead at Jarn Mound and on farmland

PARKING Limited spaces opposite church or on roadside in Sunningwell

PUBLIC TOILETS None en route

When the archaeologist Sir Arthur Evans (1851–1941) built Jarn Mound, it was with the intention of providing a panoramic view across Oxfordshire towards the neighbouring counties of Warwickshire and Berkshire. However, if Evans were to climb the steps to this noted viewpoint today, he would be dismayed to discover trees and modern housing development had radically changed the character of the landscape.

It was in 1928 that the Oxford Preservation Trust purchased 64 acres (26ha) of land here on Boars Hill in order to preserve the view of Oxford and her dreaming spires (see Walk 8). A local resident and a leading figure in the world of archaeology, renowned for his discoveries at Knossos in Crete, Evans suggested to the Trust that it go one better in an effort to preserve the view from Matthew Arnold's signal-elm, which looked towards the Berkshire Downs, the Vale of White Horse, the River Thames and Oxford.

A Mound with a View

With the support of the Trust, Evans pledged to create an artificial mound to provide a wider view of the area. For as long as anyone could remember, the site had been known locally as Jarn. This was possibly a corruption of the French word for garden.

Despite huge problems, including constant soil slippage, work on the mound was eventually finished. It took nearly three years and was completed in November 1931. The task was perfect for Evans, the epitomal archaeologist, and he revelled in the challenge of erecting a 50ft (15m) high mound. On the summit was placed the dial plate indicating the distances between the mound and significant places of interest in the area. A bowl of freshly minted coins was placed inside. But Evans didn't stop there. He was keen to enclose the mound so that it blended with its surroundings, and to achieve this his next project was to establish a wild garden of British plants, having first gained the approval of the Oxford Preservation Trust. He imported appropriate soils to allow a variety of native flora to thrive here. The pit created by the building of the mound was transformed into rock and bog gardens and a pond, which was partly re-excavated in 1992.

JARN MOUND

Most people would applaud Evans's efforts to raise Jarn Mound and so provide a magnificent viewpoint for people to enjoy, surrounded by his wild garden. While not much can be done about the housing development that, he might say, blots the landscape, the trees that were growing on the mound itself, restricting the very view it was intended to permit, have recently been cut down completely, once again allowing broad vistas.

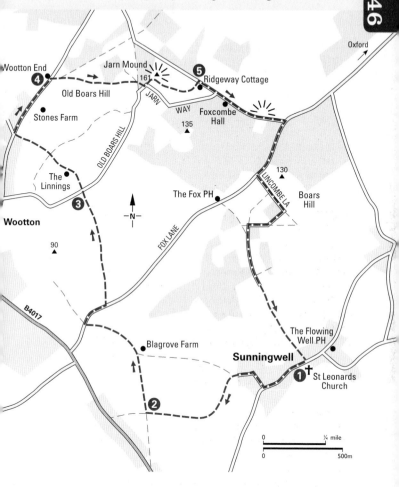

WALK 46 DIRECTIONS

1 Walk with the church on your left and, as the road bends left, turn right into Dark Lane. Beyond a school the lane becomes a concrete track but, in 50yds (46m), when it curves right, keep left, following a rough track between hedgerows and then across open fields. Didcot Power Station can be seen from here.

2 After 700yds (640m) turn right towards farm buildings and cut between them. A farm track leads out to the road 350yds (320m) distant, but the true right of way runs roughly parallel to it about 20yds (18m) to the left, in the arable field. At Fox Lane cross carefully, before the tight bend ahead! Turn right. Follow the verge for about 200yds (183m) to a sign for Old Boars Hill and take

WALK 46

the stile. Cross the open field, pass through a boundary hedge and keep ahead towards a white house. Look for a stile in the field corner beside it and cross the lane to a stile and gate.

3 Follow the metalled lane to The Linnings, a riding school. Keep to the right of the buildings, crossing three stiles. Go diagonally across the paddock, passing under power lines, to reach the boundary hedge. Cross two stiles, avoiding stiles in the left and right boundary of the field, and follow the path beside a high wire fence enclosing a reservoir. Keep ahead at the fence corner to a galvanised gate and stile on the right and follow an enclosed path beside a paddock towards the houses of Wootton. Through a galvanised gate turn right, passing the entrance to Stones Farm.

4 On reaching the entrance to Wootton End (a house) on the left, keep right here, following a track. Go through a galvanised gate and keep to the right of a pond. Take a wide fenced path uphill then cross Matthew Arnold's Field to a stile leading out to the lane. Turn left and walk along to the junction of Jarn Way and Old Boars Hill, ignoring other footpaths. Climb to Jarn Mound, then descend the steps and turn left by the seat, keeping the memorial stone on the left. Keep parallel with the road, veer left at the fork and follow the path through woodland for 250yds (229m) to the road. Turn right, pass a house (Ridgeway Cottage) and go down to the junction.

5 Go straight on, passing a side entrance to Foxcombe Hall, an Open University building. There is a clear view of the Sheldonian Theatre and many of Oxford's other historic landmarks from this stretch of the road. Walk along to the T-junction and turn right. After 400yds (366m) turn left into Lincombe Lane. Follow this good tarmac surface round to the right, pass a footpath and continue for a straight 0.25 mile (400m) to a white gate and a kissing gate. Follow the field path towards Sunningwell church. Go through a gate at the bottom of the field to finish the walk.

Greys Court – a Charm in the Chilterns

Visit a National Trust property in a delightfully unspoiled setting on this pretty walk in the Chilterns.

DISTANCE 3.5 miles (5.7km) **MINIMUM TIME** 1hr 30min	
ASCENT/GRADIENT 150ft (46m) ▲▲▲ **LEVEL OF DIFFICULTY** ✦✦✦	
PATHS Field and parkland paths, drives and tracks, stretches of road (can be busy), one short, steep section, 13 stiles	
LANDSCAPE Chiltern hills and farmland, Greys Court parkland	
SUGGESTED MAP OS Explorer 171 Chiltern Hills West	
START/FINISH Grid reference: SU 726823	
DOG FRIENDLINESS Several dog stiles; under control by golf course and on lead in vicinity of Greys Court	
PARKING Spaces by church at Rotherfield Greys	
PUBLIC TOILETS Greys Court, for visitors; otherwise none en route	

There is a charming intimacy about Greys Court, a delightfully homely air that is not always evident in properties that have been immaculately restored and preserved by the National Trust. Major conservation building work has included the restoration of the roof, chimneys and gables. This was followed by the removal of asbestos from some parts of the building, which then made it possible to install improved electrical, plumbing, and heating infrastructures, and to make smaller conservation repairs to such things as ceilings and panelling.

Romantic Ruins

The flint walls and ivy-clad towers are all that remain of a sizeable 14th-century crenellated mansion belonging to the Lords Grey of Rotherfield. Within them Sir William Knollys, Earl of Banbury, built a manor house in 1605. His father, Francis Knollys, had been treasurer to Elizabeth I. Greys Court passed to Sir William Stapleton in the 1720s. His descendants remained here until 1935.

During the time the house was occupied by the Stapletons, the estate comprised a staggering 8,000 acres (3,240ha) of woodland, parkland and farmland. Today, it covers a more modest 300 acres (121.5ha), with the delightful 16th-century house, standing beside the ruins of the old fortified manor, at its heart.

One of Greys Court's most popular attractions is its picturesque garden. When Sir Felix and Lady Brunner moved here in 1937, they found this area of the estate to be sadly neglected. War was declared soon after their arrival, so very little work was undertaken until the late 1940s. However, when it came to planning improvements to the garden, the Brunners found the old walls of the fortified manor gave them a distinct advantage over many other country houses.

The gardener's statue in the Kitchen Garden commemorates Charles Taylor, who was Head Gardener at Greys Court between 1937 and 1955.

GREYS COURT

It was he who helped Lady Brunner rescue the garden and give it new life. The iron pergola linking the Kitchen Garden and the Wisteria Garden includes the initials of Sir Felix and Lady Brunner, and was commissioned to mark their golden wedding in 1977. The wisteria has the effect of binding the various gardens and is best appreciated in early May.

The White Garden was inspired by the renowned gardens of Sissinghurst in Kent, the work of Sir Harold Nicolson and his wife, the writer Victoria (Vita) Sackville-West. This was the first garden at Greys Court to be restored; it was completed in the mid-1950s. The old glasshouse was demolished and stone slabs from the kitchen were used to pave the new summer house and terrace. The pond was created to mark a family engagement.

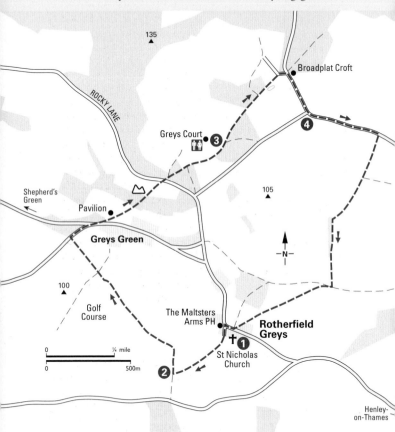

WALK 47 DIRECTIONS

1 With the St Nicholas church lychgate on your left-hand side, walk towards The Maltsters Arms pub and turn immediately left before William's Cottage to join a gravel drive. Follow the

footpath as it runs alongside the churchyard and make for the stile ahead. Then head obliquely right, across the field to another stile, go over a third stile and then veer half right in the next field. Make for a stile, cross over and join a track.

GREYS COURT

❷ Turn right and pass between trees, high hedges and margins of bracken. The track passes alongside the fairways of a golf course before crossing a drive to a gate. Continue ahead to reach the road and turn right. Pass a turning for Shepherd's Green on the left and follow the road along to the grassy expanse of Greys Green. Veer left on to the green and aim to the right of the pavilion. Join a footpath, cross a stile and descend very steeply through trees to the next stile. Pass under power lines in the pasture and keep the fence on the left. Make for a stile, cross a lane to a footpath and after a few steps you reach a stile. Take the tarmac driveway ahead for about 400yds (366m) to reach the admission kiosk to Greys Court.

❸ Veer left here, following the footpath across two pastures, and in the third take a little stile and boardwalk to cross a small pond. Pass alongside a fence and woodland, avoiding a gate and some steps to reach two stiles on the left just beyond them by a corrugated barn. Cross over the stile and keep to the right-hand side, with the fence and field on the right. Turn right at a drive and make for the road ahead. Turn right at this junction, opposite Broadplat Croft.

❹ Keep left at the next junction and continue along the road for 0.25 mile (400m) to reach a tree-lined driveway on the right, signposted to Rotherfield Greys. Where the driveway turns left keep ahead, following a rough track for 300yds (274m) to trees marking an old pit. Just beyond this take a stile (or gap) left, to follow a path down the hillside, keeping a belt of woodland on the right. Beyond it, continue on the grassy path with a fence on the right. Turn right, across a stile in the field corner, and follow the path alongside fencing. After about 60yds (55m), look for a stile on the left. Cross it, at first maintaining the same direction, but soon swinging left to follow the path up the slope and back to the road opposite the church at Rotherfield Greys where you started the walk.

Stoke Row and a Maharajah's Gift

Discover the link between India and a quiet English village on this pleasant walk in the Chilterns.

DISTANCE 4.25 miles (6.8km)	**MINIMUM TIME** 2hrs

ASCENT/GRADIENT 164ft (50m) ▲▲▲   **LEVEL OF DIFFICULTY** ✦✦✦

PATHS Field and woodland paths and tracks, road (busy), 8 stiles

LANDSCAPE Chiltern woodland and farmland

SUGGESTED MAP OS Explorer 171 Chiltern Hills West

START/FINISH Grid reference: SU 678840

DOG FRIENDLINESS On lead in Stoke Row and Cherry Orchard; under control where indicated; on lead where indicated on Walk 49

PARKING Roadside parking in Stoke Row

PUBLIC TOILETS None en route

It is unusual, to say the least, and not what you would expect to find in an English village. Enclosed by an exotic cupola, the Maharajah's Well might be a familiar landmark in Stoke Row but first-time visitors gaze curiously at this spectacle, unsure at first if they can believe what they are seeing.

The well was given to the village by the Maharajah of Benares in 1863 as a gift. But where, you might ask, is the connection with Stoke Row? It was on a Benares hillside, around the middle of the 19th century, that the Indian ruler met Edward Anderdon Reade, who was soon to become Lieutenant-Governor of the North West Provinces of India. The Maharajah indicated his plans to overcome the acute water shortage in the area and Anderdon Reade responded by pointing out that it was a familiar problem at home in the Chilterns where his father ran an estate.

A Precious Resource

In villages like Stoke Row, he told the Maharajah, local people relied on rainwater for their cooking, and so precious was it that it was often passed from one cooking pot to the next. Neighbours shared what water they could collect and children were often punished for drinking it to quench their thirst. Pond water was used for washing and when that ran out, wash day was postponed, sometimes indefinitely.

During the Indian Mutiny, Edward Anderdon Reade offered help and support to the Maharajah of Benares, who had not forgotten Stoke Row and the ongoing problem of its water supply. To express his gratitude for the Lieutenant-Governor's solidarity at a difficult time, and as a token of friendship, the Maharajah presented the village with a charitable gift.

The local Commissioners chose a suitable site in Stoke Row and the Maharajah duly approved it, recommending that construction work should commence on the wedding day of the Prince of Wales, later Edward VII. The date was 10 March 1863. Building began with the sinking of a 4ft (1.2m) wide well to a depth of 368ft (112m), more than twice the height of Nelson's Column. All the work was done by hand.

STOKE ROW

The well was officially opened 14 months later on 24 May 1864 – Queen Victoria's birthday. A condition of the gift was 'that the public should have the privilege of taking water free of charge in all time to come.'

The beneficent Maharajah did not forget the village and donated other gifts. For example, to mark the wedding of Princess Louise he created a new footpath leading to the well and also gave £200 so that the villagers could host thanksgiving celebrations. In 1906 mains water was piped to Stoke Row and in 1927 a second pipeline brought water from Nettlebed.

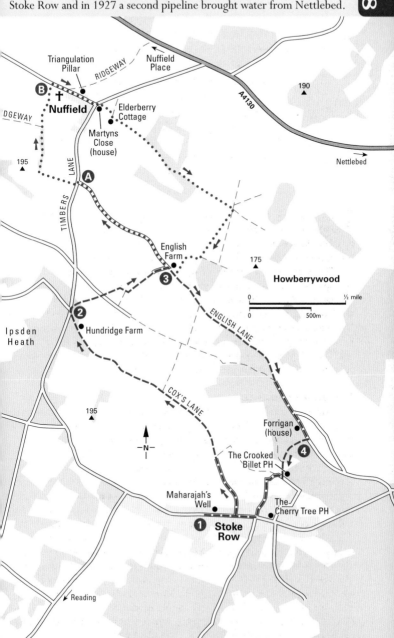

WALK 48

WALK 48 DIRECTIONS

❶ In Stoke Row walk eastwards, past the village stores. Turn left into Cox's Lane and stay on it for about a mile (1.6km). It curves to the left, then dwindles to a track. You will see an occasional waymark. The track narrows to a path, running between trees and hedgerows. Eventually you reach the outbuildings of (and unsightly debris surrounding) Hundridge Farm. Join a track running through the woodland and make for the road.

❷ Turn right along the road for 40yds (36m), then swing right at the footpath sign into the wood. Follow the path between trees and cross a drive. Make for a stile ahead and then go diagonally right in the field, using the waymark posts to guide you. Look for a

stile in the corner and cross a lane to a further stile on the opposite side. Head diagonally right in the field and look for a stile by a hard tennis court. Pass alongside a beech hedge to a drive and turn left. As the drive sweeps left to a house, go forward over a cattle grid to a field. Continue with the boundary on your left and, on reaching the corner, go straight on along a track.

❸ Turn right at English Farm and follow a sign towards Witheridge Hill, along the narrow track known as English Lane. Stay on this, later in trees, for 0.75 mile (1.2km). When you strike tarmac keep the same line. Pass a timber-framed cottage on the left-hand side and a house on the right called Forrigan. Keep ahead for about 100yds (91m) and swing right at a sign for Stoke Row.

❹ Cross a stile and cut through the wood. Emerge from the woodland at a gate and cross a pasture to more woodland. Go through another gate and, now in thin woodland, turn left, gently uphill, and cross one field. Strike the narrow lane via the car park for The Crooked Billet. Turn right for 0.25 mile (400m) to reach the crossroads in the centre of Stoke Row. Turn right and return to the start.

A Loop to Nuffield

Extend the walk to a scattered hilltop village.

See map and information panel for Walk 48

DISTANCE 2.75 miles (4.4km)   **MINIMUM TIME** 1hr 15min

ASCENT/GRADIENT 150ft (46m) ▲▲▲   **LEVEL OF DIFFICULTY** ✦✦✦

WALK 49 DIRECTIONS
(Walk 48 option)

Turn left at English Farm and follow the lane to the road junction, Point **Ⓐ**. Turn left for several paces and cross over to a footpath, following it to the left of a line of trees. Cross the field, passing under power lines, and at the far hedge go through the gap and turn right. Pass through some trees to reach the Ridgeway, which follows an earthwork, Grim's Ditch, to the west. Go straight on towards Nuffield.

Climb gently through a belt of woodland and emerge by a galvanised gate. Follow the field-edge ahead to the road and turn right, Point **Ⓑ**. Pass the 900-year-old church with its helpful sign indicating a water tap.

The church is 700ft (213m) above sea level and the highest point in the southern Chilterns. Two thousand years ago, this would have been a site of Druidic worship involving human sacrifice. The Roman invasion brought law and order, and this hilltop almost certainly became the setting for a Roman villa. Some of the tiles have been incorporated into the church tower.

The churchyard contains the grave of the renowned car manufacturer and benefactor William Morris, (1877–1963) (see Walk 9), who fell in love with this lofty village and took its name as Viscount Nuffield. He lived at nearby Nuffield Place.

Continue along the road through the village, parting company with the Ridgeway now. Between Half Acre and Old School House look carefully in the hedgerow opposite: you may just be able to make out an obsolete, grey triangulation pillar, now smothered in vegetation. Make for the junction with Timbers Lane. Cross over and pass to the left of a house called Martyns Close. Follow the path to a gravelled drive by some houses and pass Elderberry Cottage on the right.

Keep ahead on an enclosed bridleway, between trees and bushes, for 0.75 mile (1.2km). On reaching a track, turn right and after a very few paces you come to a sign for Howberrywood Farm. Cross the stile beside this sign and go diagonally right across the field, aiming for some trees just to the left of English Farm. Look for a gate leading out to a track, keep right and follow it as it curves left. Pass left of the farm outbuildings to reach a junction of tracks and then rejoin Walk 48.

Mapledurham – Screen Star

Visit a remote village used as a film and television location on this pretty walk.

DISTANCE 2.25 miles (3.6km) MINIMUM TIME 1hr

ASCENT/GRADIENT 164ft (50m) ▲▲▲ LEVEL OF DIFFICULTY ✚✚✚

PATHS *Mainly farm tracks and field paths, 3 stiles*

LANDSCAPE *Parkland and farmland on northern bank of Thames*

SUGGESTED MAP *OS Explorer 159 Reading*

START *Grid reference: SU 670767*

DOG FRIENDLINESS *On lead in Mapledurham, under control elsewhere*

PARKING *Permission kindly given for walkers to use small car park adjacent to church*

PUBLIC TOILETS *Mapledurham House, for visitors; otherwise none en route*

WALK 50 DIRECTIONS

Mapledurham and its timeless Thames setting in the south-east corner of Oxfordshire create an idyllic picture. The village is one of only a few settlements in the area that have not been blighted by urban development. The lack of a road bridge providing a direct link with nearby Reading has, in effect, ruled out the possibility of expansion, and Mapledurham remains a sleepy, rather isolated village approached down narrow winding lanes running deep into the heart of the countryside. Not surprisingly, life in this part of the world tends to be on the quiet and uneventful side.

However, it was a very different story back in 1976. If you could somehow transform yourself back in time to the very hot summer of that year you would have found Mapledurham a hive of activity. The village might have been hard to recognise too – and, even more puzzling, its name had changed to Studley Constable. An old-fashioned dairy shop displayed gleaming milk churns in the window; stirrup pumps and baby Austins added to the nostalgic picture of rural England; and, perhaps most bizzare of all, there were signposts to the east-coast port of King's Lynn.

Almost everywhere you went, there was a genuine feeling that the village had stood still since the Second World War. But why? What did it all mean? Still mystified? The clue is in the title of this walk. Mapledurham was doubling as a film set for the celluloid version of *The Eagle Has Landed*, a classic adventure yarn by thriller writer Jack Higgins. If you have read the book or seen the film, then you'll know the plot concerns

WHERE TO EAT AND DRINK

There are no inns in Mapledurham but at nearby Chazey Heath the Pack Saddle pub offers food every day. Mapledurham House has a tea room.

MAPLEDURHAM

an attempt to kidnap Winston Churchill (see Walks 21 and 22) while he is spending the weekend in Norfolk in 1943.

Much of the film, which stars Michael Caine and Donald Sutherland, was shot at Mapledurham, and the village Church of St Margaret, where the villagers are held captive, features prominently. However, if you expect to get a drink at the delightfully named Spyglass and Kettle, you'll be disappointed. The pub was a clever illusion created by film designers and artists.

WHILE YOU'RE THERE

Visit Mapledurham House, completed in the late 16th century by Sir Richard Blount for his Catholic family. Built of red brick with stone dressings, Mapledurham is one of the largest and most famous Elizabethan houses in Oxfordshire. The house contains a priest hole and there is also an 18th-century private chapel, visible from the adjacent churchyard.

Easy access to London and the success of *The Eagle Has Landed* have resulted in Mapledurham being regularly chosen as a location for film and television productions. They include *Class Act* starring Joanna Lumley, and *Inspector Morse* with the late John Thaw as the world-famous Oxford sleuth. The gently lapping Thames, imposing Mapledurham House and neat rows of handsome houses in the main street create just the right images for the large and small screen – the quintessential English village.

From the small car park by the church, turn right and walk along the village street to a bridleway on the right, signposted to Gravel Hill. Pass the lodge on the corner and a telephone box and follow the concrete track for 200yds (183m) to a stile and gate. Turn left, soon taking a stile into Park Wood. Ascend steadily, to a statue mounted on a stone plinth, itself mounted on a tall brick plinth. Continue on the path for 350yds (320m), then cross a track diagonally. In a few paces go half right to a straight track. On leaving the woodland keep ahead for another 200yds (183m), to a junction. Turn very sharply left, along Pond Lane. Follow this concrete track round several bends for a little over 0.5 mile (800m), enjoying good views over Berkshire and Oxfordshire, to Lilley Farm.

Turn left at the road and follow it for 100yds (91m) until you reach a footpath sign at the entrance to Lilley Barn on the left where the lane curves right. Behind the hedge follow the path and pass through a galvanised gate. Walk ahead to the next gate and cross the field, keeping the brick and timber-framed Step Cottage to your right. Avoid the stile leading out to the road and continue crossing the field, eventually curving to the left at the point where you see the road ahead.

The walk crosses a slope and then runs parallel with the lane leading to Mapledurham. Locate a 'Passing Place' sign and a stile below trees, but then walk 100yds (91m) further in the field to a footpath sign and a kissing gate, through which steps descend to the lane. Turn left for Mapledurham House and the village centre.

Walking in Safety

All these walks are suitable for any reasonably fit person, but less experienced walkers should try the easier walks first. Route finding is usually straightforward, but you will find that an Ordnance Survey map is a useful addition to the route maps and descriptions.

RISKS

Although each walk here has been researched with a view to minimising the risks to the walkers who follow its route, no walk in the countryside can be considered to be completely free from risk. Walking in the outdoors will always require a degree of common sense and judgement to ensure that it is as safe as possible.

- Be particularly careful on cliff paths and in upland terrain, where the consequences of a slip can be very serious.

- Remember to check tidal conditions before walking on the seashore.

- Some sections of route are by, or cross, busy roads. Take care and remember traffic is a danger even on minor country lanes.

- Be careful around farmyard machinery and livestock, especially if you have children with you.

- Be aware of the consequences of changes in the weather and check the forecast before you set out. Carry spare clothing and a torch if you are walking in the winter months. Remember the weather can change very quickly at any time of the year, and in moorland and heathland areas, mist and fog can make route finding much harder. Don't set out in these conditions unless you are confident of your navigation skills in poor visibility. In summer remember to take account of the heat and sun; wear a hat and carry spare water.

- On walks away from centres of population you should carry a whistle and survival bag. If you do have an accident requiring the emergency services, make a note of your position as accurately as possible and dial 999.

COUNTRYSIDE CODE

- Be safe, plan ahead and follow any signs.

- Leave gates and property as you find them.

- Protect plants and animals and take your litter home.

- Keep dogs under close control.

- Consider other people.

For more information visit www.countrysideaccess.gov.uk/things_to_know/countryside_code